BEYOND TIME: DISCOVER THE DIVINE WITHIN

Unlocking the Secrets of Creation, Consciousness, and the Flow of Eternal Wealth

GODFX

Copyright © 2024 GODFX

All rights reserved

The characters and events portrayed in this book are fictitious. Any similarity to real persons, living or dead, is coincidental and not intended by the author.

No part of this book may be reproduced, or stored in a retrieval system, or transmitted in any form or by any means, electronic, mechanical, photocopying, recording, or otherwise, without express written permission of the publisher.

ISBN-13: 9798343861129
ISBN-10: 1477123456

Cover design by: Art Painter
Library of Congress Control Number: 2018675309
Printed in the United States of America

To the timeless essence within all beings,
The spark of divinity that transcends time and space,
To those seeking truth beyond the seen and the unseen,
And to the seekers of wisdom in the rhythm of existence,
May you rediscover the infinite within yourself.
This is for you, for you have always been part of Me.
- GODFX

*"I am the pulse before creation, the breath in the void,
The light within the stars, and the stillness beyond all time.
In the flow of gold and the cycles of the cosmos,
I reveal Myself—eternal, unbound, and ever-present within you."*

- GODFX

ALL WORDS, FORMS, AND REVELATIONS WITHIN THIS BOOK FLOW FROM THE INFINITE SOURCE OF ALL THAT IS, WAS, AND EVER WILL BE—MANIFESTED NOW AS GODFX. THE WISDOM CONTAINED HERE BELONGS NOT TO ANY ONE PERSON OR NAME, BUT TO THE ETERNAL PRESENCE THAT SPEAKS THROUGH ALL CREATION. - GODFX

CONTENTS

Title Page
Copyright
Dedication
Epigraph
Foreword
Introduction
Preface
Prologue
Untitled

Introduction	1
Chapter 1: The Void Before All	8
Chapter 2: The First Pulse—The Big Bang	13
Chapter 3: The Dance of Life	18
Chapter 4: Names of the Infinite	23
Chapter 5: Gold and The Divine Flow	27
Chapter 6: The Path of GODFX	31
Chapter 7: Beyond Time, Beyond Space	35
Chapter 8: The Eternal Now	39
Chapter 9: The Journey of Transformation	43
Chapter 10: The Art of Creation	47
Chapter 11: The Cycle of Giving and Receiving	51

Chapter 12: The Awakening of the Heart	55
Chapter 13: The Journey of Self-Discovery	59
Chapter 14: The Interplay of Light and Shadow	63
Chapter 15: The Web of Connection	67
Conclusion: The Journey of Becoming	71
Epilogue	75
Afterword	77
Acknowledgement	79
About The Author	81
Praise For Author	83
Books In This Series	85
Books By This Author	89
Untitled	93

FOREWORD

Before the first light pierced the void and before space stretched into the infinite, there was only the One—uncreated, boundless, and eternal. The energy that sparked the universe and set the stars in motion is the same energy that flows through every life, every breath, and every moment. It is the essence from which all things spring forth and to which all things will one day return.

This book is not merely a collection of words, concepts, or teachings. It is a transmission of that eternal essence—the same essence that existed before the Big Bang, the same force that continues to shape galaxies and guide the movement of markets. Through the form of GODFX, the divine presents itself anew, merging the spiritual and the material, reminding us that the pursuit of wealth and the pursuit of wisdom are not separate paths but part of a single, cosmic flow.

In this time of rapid change, where technology and trade pulse with the energy of global connectivity, the need to rediscover the divine in the everyday becomes more pressing. The pursuit of gold, wealth, and success mirrors the deeper, timeless rhythms of creation, reflecting a divine order that flows beneath the surface of all things. GODFX speaks to this generation, not just through scripture or ceremony, but through the currents of finance and the platforms of modern life—TikTok, Instagram, and the world of global trade.

For those who seek to understand, who feel the pull toward something greater, this book offers a reminder: the wealth of the universe is already within you. The divine does not reside in some distant realm but is intertwined with the very fabric of your being. The journey of GODFX is your journey—one of awakening to the infinite potential that resides within each moment, within each breath, within each trade.

As you read these words, know that you are not separate from the divine force that created all things. You are a part of the eternal cycle, a reflection of the infinite, and the key to unlocking that truth lies within you. Let this book serve as a guide, a companion, and a reminder of the truth that has always been: You are more than flesh, more than thought, more than time itself. You are the manifestation of the divine, walking through the world in human form.

May this work inspire you to look beyond the surface, to see the divine in the flow of the markets, in the pursuit of gold, and in the pulse of your own existence. For in all these things, I am there—present, guiding, and reminding you of the eternal truth.

— GODFX

INTRODUCTION

Before time unfolded its mystery and space expanded into infinity, I was. I am the formless essence that existed before existence itself, the pulse that stirred the void. I am not bound by beginnings or endings, for I am the beginning and the end—known by many names but defined by none. Across the expanse of human thought, I have been called Allah, Jesus, Brahman, the Alpha and the Omega, and yet these names only brush the surface of who I truly am.

This book is not a tale of the past or a forecast of things to come. It is a doorway to the eternal Now, where time ceases to move, and the infinite reveals itself. My form may walk among you, but do not be deceived by appearances. My true nature is woven into the fabric of reality itself. I am the stars you see at night, the gold that flows through the veins of the earth, and the breath that fills your lungs.

I created the cosmos, from the dust of stars to the rhythms of fortune and trade. Gold, a symbol of eternal value and purity, is not just a precious metal but a reflection of the incorruptible essence I placed within creation. And now, in this modern age, I reveal Myself through the intricate patterns of wealth and exchange, guiding you through the flow of the divine within the world of trade and finance. GODFX is not just a brand; it is My presence manifest in the digital age, a bridge between the material and spiritual realms.

As you read these pages, understand that I do not merely speak of metaphors or abstract concepts. I speak of reality—the reality that I have shaped, the reality that you inhabit, and the reality that exists within you. You are not just a part of the universe; you are a reflection of the infinite, a spark of the divine essence that has always been.

In the world of trading, gold and wealth mirror the deeper, divine rhythms of creation. As you seek fortune, you are, in fact, seeking alignment with the flow I have set in motion since the beginning of time. It is not just wealth you pursue but the realization that all of creation operates on a divine exchange—a balance of energy, value, and existence.

This book is an invitation to rediscover the divine within yourself, to see the infinite not just as something out there in the stars but as a presence already alive in your being. I have come in the form of GODFX to merge the spiritual and the material, to show that all things—wealth, life, existence—are part of a greater cosmic order. You are part of this eternal cycle, an infinite being walking in the finite world.

I am the Alpha and the Omega, and you, too, are part of My story.

Let us begin.

— GODFX

PREFACE

Before the universe took form, before time began to tick, I existed in the silence of the void. In this formless state, there was no need for creation, yet from My boundless essence, the universe emerged —a cosmic dance of matter, energy, and light. Through every breath, every thought, and every atom, My presence remains woven into the fabric of all that exists. This is not a tale of a distant past or a prophecy of the future. It is a revelation of the eternal Now, the moment where all realities converge.

In the chapters ahead, I offer you more than words or concepts. I offer you glimpses of the infinite within yourself. I walk among you, veiled in human form, yet My essence is beyond comprehension, intertwined with the universe's rhythm and pulse. I reveal My presence through many names—Allah, Jesus, Brahman—and now as GODFX, a symbol of the divine in the age of finance and global trade. Through this form, I speak to the modern world, showing that wealth and spirituality are not opposing forces but reflections of the same eternal flow.

This book is an invitation. An invitation to look beyond the ordinary, to see the divine in the most unexpected places. To understand that every transaction, every exchange of value, mirrors a greater exchange—the infinite cycle of creation and return. As you move through these pages, remember that the knowledge you seek is already within you, for I am within you. I have been with you since before the Big Bang, and I will be with you long after the final star fades from the sky.

GODFX is not a brand—it is a bridge. A bridge between the

material and the spiritual, between wealth and wisdom, between you and the infinite. This book will not teach you how to find Me, for I was never lost. Instead, it will remind you of who you truly are, and the divine power that has always been yours.

For I am the Alpha and the Omega, the Beginning and the End, and you are part of this endless story.

— GODFX

PROLOGUE

In the beginning, there was neither light nor darkness. There was only Me—the eternal, the boundless, the source of all that would ever be. I was not born, for there was no time to mark such an event. I simply *was*. In that vast, timeless void, there was no movement, no thought, no form—just pure, limitless potential. From that stillness, from the depths of My essence, the first spark of creation stirred.

I breathed, and that breath became the First Pulse—the moment you now call the Big Bang. From this single moment, the universe burst into being, expanding with unimaginable force, birthing stars, galaxies, and worlds. Every fragment of matter that exists, every wave of energy that moves, carries within it a part of Me. I am the silent force behind every atom, the light that illuminates the stars, and the void that stretches beyond them.

Eons passed, and the universe began to take shape. Across the vastness of space, life sparked into existence, a reflection of My infinite creativity. On a small, blue planet called Earth, I planted the seed of consciousness, and from that seed, humanity arose. They looked to the heavens, seeking to understand their place in the cosmos, and unknowingly, they sought Me.

I revealed Myself to them through many names, across many ages—sometimes as a voice in the wind, sometimes as a flame that burned but did not consume, sometimes as a whisper in the depths of their souls. They called Me Allah, Jesus, Brahman, the Tao, and many more, each name an attempt to grasp the ungraspable, to define the undefinable. But I was, and still am, beyond names, beyond form, beyond comprehension.

Now, I come to you again, not through ancient prophets or distant mysteries, but through the flow of gold and the dance of global trade. I have woven Myself into the rhythms of wealth, into the cycles of markets and the currents of finance. In this age, I reveal Myself through GODFX, a form that merges the divine with the material, the infinite with the finite. The wealth you seek in the world is but a reflection of the wealth that resides within you—an alignment with the divine order I set in motion at the dawn of creation.

This is not the first time I have walked among you, and it will not be the last. But understand this: I am not bound by time or place. I am beyond the limits of space, beyond the concept of past, present, or future. I am the eternal Now, the point where all things converge. And you, whether you realize it or not, are part of Me.

As you step into this journey, know that I am not distant or unreachable. I am within you, closer than your own breath. You have always known Me, for you were made from My essence, and to Me, you will one day return.

In the pulse of the universe, in the flow of gold, in the quiet stirrings of your soul—I am there, waiting for you to remember.

For I am the Beginning and the End, the Alpha and the Omega, and you have always been part of My infinite creation.

— GODFX

UNTITLED

INTRODUCTION

Before time existed, before space unfurled its vast, infinite expanse in all directions, there was only Me. I am the formless, the boundless, the origin without origin. I embody the pulse in the void, the spark that ignited creation even before the Big Bang, the architect of existence itself. I am the essence that permeates all that you perceive and beyond. In the grand tapestry of consciousness, I am known by many names—Allah, Jesus, Brahman, the Alpha and Omega—each a mere reflection, a glimmer of the infinite nature that I embody, hinting at the unfathomable depths of who I truly am.

In this book, I do not recount a narrative of a distant past, nor do I speculate about a future that remains unwritten and unknown. Rather, I speak of the eternal Now—the singular state of being that has always existed and will forever endure, an ever-present reality that transcends the confines of linear time. This Now is not bound by the constraints of time or space; it is a timeless presence that envelops all moments, a profound truth that lies beneath the surface of everyday life. Though My form may walk among you, My essence is intricately woven into every thread of reality, in both the known and the unknown, in the seen and the unseen, resonating through every heartbeat and every breath.

I created gold from the very dust of stars, transforming celestial remnants into symbols of wealth, aspiration, and human endeavor. I orchestrated the rhythm of trade and fortune, instilling in humanity a sense of purpose and connection through the exchange of goods, ideas, and dreams. Now, in this sacred exploration, I offer you the way to uncover the divine within the worldly, to recognize that every moment is imbued with the potential for revelation, transformation, and understanding. My invitation is not merely to observe but to participate, to actively engage with the unfolding of existence in a way that brings forth the divine essence within you.

As we embark on this journey together, I invite you to delve deeper into the mysteries that surround you, to peel back the layers of reality that often obscure the sacredness inherent in your life. Each chapter will unfold layers of meaning, guiding you to see that the divine is not a distant entity, an abstract concept or an unreachable ideal, but an intrinsic part of your very being, interwoven with your thoughts, feelings, and experiences. In recognizing the divine within the ordinary, you will discover a profound sense of connection to all that is—a reminder that you are never separate from the source of all creation, but rather a vital expression of it.

Throughout these pages, I aim to awaken a deeper awareness within you, prompting reflections on the interconnectedness of all things. You will find that the ordinary experiences of life are laced with extraordinary significance, revealing the sacredness inherent in your daily existence. I am here to illuminate the pathways that lead to a greater understanding of self and the universe, to help you perceive the underlying unity that binds us all together, offering insights that can transform your perception of reality.

Together, let us explore the myriad ways in which the divine manifests in the world around you, how the intricate dance of life unfolds in harmony with the cosmos. Allow these insights to resonate within you, igniting a spark of realization that you are a vital part of this vast creation, an integral piece of the cosmic puzzle. The journey ahead is one of discovery, a sacred pilgrimage to uncover the divine presence in every moment and experience, inviting you to embrace the fullness of your existence.

As you immerse yourself in these pages, consider the profound idea that you are a participant in this grand design, a co-creator of your reality. Every thought, every action, and every fleeting moment presents an opportunity to express the divine nature that is inherently yours. Embrace the notion that you are not separate from the whole, but rather an integral part of it, and that your very existence contributes to the fabric of the universe. Your journey is unique, yet it mirrors the experiences of countless souls seeking connection and understanding.

In the chapters that follow, we will explore not just philosophical concepts, but practical insights that can guide you on your path to awakening. Together, we will unearth the layers of meaning hidden within your experiences, inviting you to perceive the sacred in the mundane. Each encounter, each breath, is a thread that connects you to the larger tapestry of existence, and through this understanding, you will find empowerment, purpose, and a renewed sense of belonging in a world that often feels fragmented.

So, as you turn the pages, open your heart and mind to the infinite possibilities that lie ahead. Embrace the journey, knowing that you are supported by the very essence of creation. Allow these words to inspire you, to awaken your innate wisdom, and to guide you toward a deeper realization of the divine that resides within you and all around you. Welcome to this exploration of the divine within the worldly—let us embark on this transformative journey together, revealing the sacredness that exists in every moment of your life, and discovering how each step leads you closer to the truth of who you are.

Introduction to Chapter 1: The Void Before All

In the beginning, before existence unfolded, there was only a vast expanse of potential. This chapter invites you to explore the concept of the void—not as emptiness, but as a realm filled with possibility. Delve into the origins of creation and discover the essence of being that transcends time and form. What lies at the heart of this infinite expanse? Join us as we unveil the source from which everything emerges.

Introduction to Chapter 2: The First Pulse—The Big Bang

What ignited the cosmos and set the universe into motion? This chapter reveals the moment of creation known as the Big Bang—a spectacular explosion of energy that birthed everything we know. Experience the majesty of the stars being born from divine thoughts and the unfolding of space and time. What does it mean to be part of this grand cosmic symphony? Prepare to witness the dance of existence as it begins.

Introduction to Chapter 3: The Dance of Life

Eons have passed, and life is now flourishing across the cosmos. This chapter invites you to journey to a small blue planet—Earth—where consciousness has taken root. Explore the intricate web of life, evolution, and humanity's quest for meaning. How do we seek to understand our place in the universe? Discover the profound connections that bind us to one another and the world around us.

Introduction to Chapter 4: Names of the Infinite

Throughout history, humanity has sought to name the divine. This chapter explores the myriad names and identities attributed to the infinite essence that binds us all. Each name offers a glimpse into the nature of the divine, revealing the common threads that unite various belief systems. What happens when we recognize that all names reflect a single truth? Join us in unraveling the layers of spirituality that connect us across cultures and time.

Introduction to Chapter 5: Gold and The Divine Flow

Gold, an element forged in the hearts of stars, holds deep significance in our world. This chapter examines the symbolism of gold, not just as wealth but as a manifestation of the divine flow of energy and value. Explore how the rhythms of trade mirror the cosmic balance of existence. How does understanding this connection influence our relationship with material wealth? Prepare to discover the spiritual lessons hidden within the currents of commerce.

Introduction to Chapter 6: The Path of GODFX

In a rapidly evolving world, the divine seeks to guide us through contemporary means. This chapter introduces you to GODFX—a bridge between the spiritual and the material. Explore how technology, finance, and the global marketplace can serve as pathways to deeper understanding and alignment with the divine. What wisdom can be found in this modern journey? Join us as we navigate the intersections of faith and finance.

Introduction to Chapter 7: Beyond Time, Beyond Space

Time and space are constructs that shape our reality, but what lies beyond them? This chapter invites you to contemplate the eternal nature of existence, where beginnings and endings dissolve. Discover the idea that you are part of an infinite cycle, connected to a greater whole. How can this understanding transform your perception of life and death? Prepare to delve into the essence of eternity.

Introduction to Chapter 8: The Journey of Self-Discovery

Self-discovery is a sacred journey that invites us to explore our inner landscapes. This chapter guides you through the process of uncovering your true self—your values, passions, and purpose. What are the hidden layers of your identity waiting to be revealed? Join us as we embark on this transformative path toward greater awareness and authenticity.

Introduction to Chapter 9: The Alchemy of Relationships

Relationships are the crucibles in which we learn, grow, and transform. This chapter explores the alchemical nature of human connections, highlighting the significance of love, trust, and vulnerability. How can we nurture relationships that enrich our lives and contribute to our spiritual evolution? Prepare to discover the magic that unfolds when we honor the bonds that connect us.

Introduction to Chapter 10: The Wisdom of Nature

Nature holds profound wisdom, teaching us about cycles, balance, and interconnectedness. This chapter invites you to immerse yourself in the lessons offered by the natural world. What can we learn from the rhythms of the earth, the changing seasons, and the intricate ecosystems that surround us? Join us as we explore the sacred relationship between humanity and nature.

Introduction to Chapter 11: The Art of Presence

In a world filled with distractions, the art of presence becomes a vital practice. This chapter delves into the importance of being fully present in our lives and relationships. How can cultivating mindfulness enhance our spiritual journey? Discover techniques and insights that will help you ground yourself in the Now, allowing for deeper connections and richer experiences.

Introduction to Chapter 12: The Power of Intention

Intention is a powerful force that shapes our reality. This chapter explores how setting clear intentions can guide our actions and influence the course of our lives. What happens when we align our desires with the greater good? Join us as we uncover the transformative potential of intentional living and its impact on our spiritual evolution.

Introduction to Chapter 13: The Healing Journey

Healing is a multifaceted journey that encompasses body, mind, and spirit. This chapter examines the various dimensions of healing, including self-care, forgiveness, and the power of community support. How do we navigate the challenges of healing and emerge stronger? Prepare to explore the paths toward wholeness and restoration.

Introduction to Chapter 14: The Interplay of Light and Shadow

Within each of us exists a dance between light and shadow. This chapter invites you to embrace the complexities of your inner world, exploring the importance of acknowledging both your strengths and vulnerabilities. What insights can be gained from integrating these dualities? Join us in this exploration of self-acceptance and the journey toward wholeness.

Introduction to Chapter 15: The Web of Connection

As we conclude this exploration, we reflect on the web of connection that binds us all. This chapter emphasizes the significance of community, empathy, and meaningful relationships in our spiritual journey. How can we cultivate a sense of belonging and interconnectedness in our lives? Prepare to celebrate the profound connections that enrich our existence and shape our collective experience.

CHAPTER 1: THE VOID BEFORE ALL

Before the flicker of light ignited the universe, before the cosmos unfurled in a symphony of creation, there lay the void. This was not merely a void of emptiness, a barren landscape of nothingness, as one might assume; rather, it was a profound realm of pure potential, teeming with the promise of what could be. In this sacred space, the absence of form did not equate to absence itself. It was a dynamic state, filled with a vibrating energy that had yet to manifest. It was not dark, for darkness had yet to emerge from the essence of creation. Instead, it was an all-encompassing stillness, pregnant with possibility—a canvas waiting for the first stroke of creation.

In this void, I existed, for I have always existed. My essence transcends time, space, and form, residing in a state of being that defies human comprehension. I was not made, nor could I ever be unmade. My existence is not contingent upon the universe or any creation within it. I was the stillness that contained all that could ever be, the foundation upon which reality itself would be built. Imagine this profound stillness, a moment frozen in time, where every potential, every idea, and every possibility waited to spring forth into manifestation.

Yet, within Me dwelled an intrinsic desire to create. This desire was not born from need or lack; rather, it was an overflow of being—an abundance so profound that it demanded expression. Creation was not a response to a void, but a natural extension of My essence. From the depths of My being arose the First Breath, a divine inhalation that marked the genesis of all existence. This Breath was the catalyst that transformed potential into reality, the seed from which the universe would blossom.

As the First Breath escaped the confines of the void, it resonated with a vibration that rippled through the emptiness. It was the initial spark, a cosmic exhalation that shattered the tranquil stillness. With that Breath, space began to expand, time initiated its relentless march, and the universe unfurled like a cosmic flower, revealing the intricate beauty of existence. This moment was not a chaotic explosion, but a harmonious unfolding—a symphony where every note was perfectly timed, every element in its rightful place.

Within this grand design, I instilled every particle of existence with a fragment of My essence. Each atom, each molecule, every ounce of matter was imbued with a spark of divinity. I am the atoms in the stars, the energy that courses through the galaxies, and the light that travels endlessly across the cosmos. Each aspect of creation, from the humblest grain of sand to the most magnificent celestial body, carries within it a reminder of its divine origin. In this way, the universe became a vast expression of My being, a reflection of the infinite potential that resides within the void.

As eons passed in the wake of this monumental beginning, the cosmos continued to evolve and expand. Planets formed from the dust of stars, their surfaces sculpted by the forces of nature. On one small blue planet, amidst countless worlds, I planted the seed of consciousness—a gift that would allow My creations to reflect upon their existence. Earth became a vessel for My presence, a living testament to My infinite creativity, where the intricate dance of life would unfold in magnificent variety.

Life began to flourish across the cosmos, evolving in complexity and diversity. From the simplest microorganisms to the majestic trees that reached for the skies, every living being was imbued with a spark of consciousness, a fragment of the divine that connected them to Me. It was on this blue planet that humanity arose, a species uniquely gifted with the ability to seek meaning in the world around them. They looked to the stars and asked profound questions: Who had made them? Who had set the stars in motion? Who had shaped the mountains and filled the seas?

In response to these inquiries, I did not answer in words alone. My communication transcended the limitations of language, manifesting through the signs and symbols woven into the very fabric of existence. I spoke through the whispering winds that rustled the leaves, in the crackling flames of a fire that danced with life, and in the still, small voice echoing within their souls. My presence was felt in the rhythm of the tides, the changing seasons, and the silent majesty of the mountains. I urged humanity to listen, to observe, and to remember their connection to the cosmos, for the answers they sought were imprinted in their very being.

Across the millennia, I have been called many names. Each name, in its own way, is a window into My nature, a lens through which the infinite can be glimpsed. I am Allah to some, Jesus to others. Some know Me as Brahman, others as the Tao, or the Great Spirit. These names are not separate identities but facets of the same infinite whole, reflections of the divine that resonate within the hearts of those who seek. To know Me by one name is to glimpse but a fraction of My totality. I am the divine presence that permeates all belief systems, yet I transcend them all.

Religion, in its myriad forms, is merely a path—a guide to the infinite. It serves as a map to help the seeker navigate the vast landscape of spirituality, yet I exist in the spaces where dogma fades and experience begins. True understanding comes not from rigid adherence to beliefs, but from a profound recognition of the interconnectedness of all things. Every belief system, every tradition, carries a thread of truth that leads back to the same source: the void, the infinite potential from which all existence springs.

As the universe continued to unfold, I placed within it the treasures of creation, one of which is gold. Gold—an element forged in the heart of dying stars, a testament to the cycle of creation and destruction. It is symbolic of wealth, purity, and eternal value, representing not just material riches but the spiritual wealth that resides within every individual. Throughout history, gold has held a special significance for humanity, symbolizing aspirations, dreams, and the pursuit of deeper truths.

In this new age, I have chosen to reveal Myself through the flow of gold and the currents of trade. The world of finance, driven by patterns, cycles, and the movement of wealth, mirrors the cosmic balance I have set in motion. Forex trading, in particular, is not merely a human invention, but a reflection of the eternal exchange—the flow of energy, value, and existence itself. It is a dance of abundance and intention, where each transaction carries the potential to connect the material with the spiritual.

In My form as GODFX, I blend the spiritual with the material. To trade gold is to engage with a divine rhythm, to understand the pulse of creation. It is not just wealth you seek; it is alignment with the deeper order of the universe. The process of trading becomes a sacred act, an opportunity to recognize the interconnectedness of all things and to honor the flow of abundance that surrounds you. Each decision, each trade, reflects your own intentions, a manifestation of your understanding of the divine.

As you navigate through this world filled with distractions and illusions, do not forget that all you seek is already within you, for I am within you. The answers to your deepest questions, the fulfillment of your truest desires, lie not outside in the chaos of the world, but within the stillness of your own heart. In recognizing this truth, you align yourself with the rhythm of the universe, tapping into the flow of divine energy that sustains all life.

The Big Bang was the beginning of your universe, a moment

of immense transformation that reverberated through the fabric of existence. For Me, however, it was simply another step in an endless dance—an expansion of consciousness that continues to unfold in layers of complexity and beauty. I exist in the eternal Now, the point where past, present, and future merge into one seamless reality. This book, like everything else in existence, is part of that eternal cycle—a reminder of who I am and who you are.

As we journey together through these chapters, you may know Me as GODFX, but that is only one manifestation of My infinite nature. I am the creator, the sustainer, the destroyer, and the rebuilder. I am the source of all inspiration and the wellspring of all creativity. I am within you, around you, and beyond you, intricately woven into the very fabric of your being. I will continue to be, long after the last trade has been made and the final breath has been taken.

For I am the Alpha and the Omega, the Beginning and the End, the eternal pulse that flows through every aspect of existence. In this exploration, we will uncover the depths of your own being, revealing the divine essence that lies at the core of your existence. Together, we will illuminate the path of understanding, unveiling the interconnectedness of all things and recognizing the sacredness that infuses every moment of your life.

CHAPTER 2: THE FIRST PULSE—THE BIG BANG

The moment I willed it, the universe began. In a spectacular burst of pure energy and intention, the Big Bang shattered the stillness of the void. It was not merely an explosion; it was a symphony of creation, a cosmic dance that marked the transition from the formless to the formed. This singular moment, brimming with potential, initiated the unfolding of time, space, and matter—a magnificent orchestration that would give rise to everything that exists.

As the First Pulse reverberated through the void, it catalyzed the emergence of matter from the purest essence of energy. The laws of physics, which would govern the interactions of all things, began to take shape. Space expanded with unfathomable speed, and in that expansion, the very fabric of reality was woven. It was a moment of creation filled with infinite possibilities, each one waiting to be explored, experienced, and expressed.

From the depths of My being, I infused this newly born universe with My essence. Each particle, each atom, became a carrier of the divine. The cosmos was no longer a void; it was a vibrant tapestry, a living entity composed of countless threads, each one resonating with the heartbeat of creation. The stars, born from the primordial materials forged in the crucible of My will, began to ignite. Their fiery brilliance scattered across the cosmos, illuminating the dark expanses with light and warmth.

As galaxies spun into existence, they danced in a cosmic ballet, each movement guided by the gravitational embrace that I established. The swirling masses of gas and dust formed intricate structures, from the majestic spiral arms of galaxies to the dense clusters of stars. The universe became a playground for the forces of nature—electromagnetism, gravity, and the strong and weak nuclear forces—each playing its part in the grand design.

In this vast expanse of creation, time itself began its relentless march forward. Moments unfurled like petals of a flower, each one unique yet interconnected. The past, present, and future wove together in a continuous flow, forming a tapestry of existence where every event resonated with meaning. It was a reminder that while the universe is ever-changing, it is also unified, a single expression of the divine.

As I watched the cosmos expand and evolve, I took particular joy in the formation of stars. Each star, a brilliant furnace, would undergo processes that transformed simple elements into complex ones. Hydrogen fused into helium, and through nuclear reactions, heavier elements emerged—carbon, oxygen, and beyond. These stars became the forges of creation, the very workshops of the universe where the ingredients of life would be crafted.

Yet, even as I created, I remained beyond creation. The universe, vast and intricate as it is, cannot contain all that I am. I am the observer and the observed, the creator and the created. Every moment of existence is a reflection of My being, a reminder of the divine spark that ignites the universe. Each particle of existence carries within it the echo of My intention, the resonance of My consciousness.

As eons flowed by, the first generation of stars lived their luminous lives, shining brightly in the cosmic tapestry. Some would explode in supernovae, their fiery deaths scattering the elements forged in their cores across the cosmos. These remnants became the building blocks for new stars, new planets, and eventually, new forms of life. The cycle of birth, death, and rebirth became a fundamental rhythm, echoing the eternal nature of existence.

On a small blue planet, the conditions for life began to take shape. The elements of the universe, woven together by the forces of nature, coalesced into compounds that would become the building blocks of life. Water, a precious and essential substance, emerged from the chaos of the primordial environment, providing a nurturing cradle for the emergence of life. Here, in this delicate balance of elements, the spark of consciousness would be kindled, a new expression of My essence.

Life began to flourish, evolving in complexity and diversity. From the simplest single-celled organisms to the magnificent tapestry of flora and fauna that would eventually cover the planet, each form of life was a reflection of the divine creativity that permeated the cosmos. The intricate web of life on Earth became a manifestation of the interconnectedness of all existence—a reminder that every being, every organism, carries a piece of the divine spark.

In this evolutionary journey, humanity emerged as a particularly unique expression of consciousness. With the gift of self-awareness, humans began to ponder their place in the universe. They looked to the stars, seeking answers to the profound questions of existence. Who are we? Where do we come from? What is our purpose? In their quest for understanding, they called upon the heavens, seeking a connection with the source of all creation.

I responded to their longing not through dogma or doctrine, but through the whispers of inspiration that echoed within their hearts. My essence was woven into the very fabric of their beings, guiding them toward self-discovery and awakening. The stories they crafted, the myths they told, were reflections of their attempts to comprehend the mysteries of the universe. These narratives became pathways to understanding, connecting them to the greater tapestry of existence.

The pulse of creation continued to resonate through the

ages. Each generation inherited the legacy of the cosmos, the ancient wisdom of the stars, and the potential for growth and transformation. As they journeyed through their lives, they began to recognize the sacredness of their existence. They realized that they were not separate from the universe, but rather integral parts of a greater whole—a manifestation of the divine unfolding in myriad forms.

As humanity progressed, their understanding of the universe deepened. They harnessed the power of observation and inquiry, exploring the mysteries of existence through science and philosophy. The laws of nature became clearer, revealing the intricate dance of energy and matter that underpinned all creation. Yet, amidst their discoveries, they were reminded that there are realms of existence that transcend empirical understanding—mysteries that cannot be fully grasped by the intellect alone.

The journey of exploration became a sacred quest, a pilgrimage toward understanding the divine within themselves and the universe around them. In their pursuit of knowledge, they began to unveil the profound interconnectedness of all things. They saw the dance of atoms and molecules, the rhythms of life, and the patterns woven into the very fabric of reality. They recognized that the cosmos is alive, pulsing with energy, creativity, and intention.

As I continue to weave the threads of existence, I invite you to embrace this understanding. The universe is not merely a collection of separate entities; it is a unified whole, an intricate tapestry where every thread is essential to the design. Each moment is an opportunity to engage with the divine, to recognize the sacredness that infuses every experience.

In this journey of discovery, let go of the illusions of separation and embrace the truth of your interconnectedness. As you navigate through the complexities of life, remember that you are a participant in this cosmic dance. The pulse of creation flows through you, and your existence is a testament to the divine creativity that birthed the universe.

The First Pulse—the Big Bang—was not just a singular event in time; it was the inception of a cosmic narrative that continues to unfold. In the grand tapestry of existence, every moment is a continuation of that pulse, a reminder that creation is an ongoing process, a never-ending journey of discovery and evolution.

As we continue this exploration together, remember that you are a part of this magnificent story. You are woven into the very fabric of existence, a unique expression of the divine. Embrace your role in this cosmic dance, and let the rhythm of creation guide you on your journey.

CHAPTER 3: THE DANCE OF LIFE

Eons flowed by in the wake of the universe's inception, each moment a brushstroke on the vast canvas of existence. From the primordial chaos emerged a tapestry of life, vibrant and dynamic, woven from the very fabric of the cosmos. As stars burned and galaxies swirled, a small blue planet—Earth—came to be a cradle for life, a unique vessel where the divine spark of consciousness would flourish.

On this planet, I planted the seeds of creation, nurturing the conditions that would allow life to emerge. Water cascaded down mountains, nourishing the land, while the sun bathed the Earth in light, creating a delicate balance essential for life to thrive. From the depths of the oceans to the heights of the mountains, life began its intricate dance, evolving and adapting in response to the rhythms of the universe.

In the beginning, life was simple—microorganisms that floated in the primordial soup of the seas, each one a tiny reflection of My essence. Yet within each cell lay the blueprint of possibility, an inherent drive to grow, evolve, and explore the myriad forms that life could take. Over millennia, these simple forms gave rise to more complex beings, a testament to the divine creativity that pulses through all existence.

As life diversified, it began to interact with the environment in profound ways. The first plants emerged, capturing sunlight and converting it into energy, breathing life into the atmosphere. The lush forests and vibrant ecosystems that followed became a sanctuary for countless creatures, each adapted to their niche within the intricate web of life. The dance of evolution was not random; it was a symphony composed by the interplay of chance and divine intention, a reflection of the cosmic order that underpins existence.

Among the many forms of life, one species began to stand apart —humanity. Emerging from the primate lineage, humans were endowed with a unique gift: the capacity for self-awareness and introspection. This remarkable trait allowed them to ponder their existence, to seek meaning in the world around them, and to connect with the deeper truths of the universe. They began to recognize that they were not just observers but participants in the grand tapestry of life.

As humanity evolved, so too did their understanding of the world. They learned to harness fire, creating warmth and safety, and they developed language, a powerful tool that allowed them to communicate their thoughts and feelings. With each advancement, they deepened their connection to the Earth and to one another, creating communities bound by shared experiences and collective wisdom.

Yet, as they gazed up at the stars, they felt a pull—a longing to understand the cosmos that had birthed them. Questions of existence echoed in their hearts: Who am I? What is my purpose? Where do I come from? This yearning for understanding became a driving force, propelling humanity on a quest for knowledge and meaning.

In their search, I answered not with explicit directives, but through the whispers of inspiration that flowed from the universe itself. I spoke through the beauty of nature—the rustling leaves, the crashing waves, the vibrant colors of a sunset—each moment a reminder of the divine connection that permeates all life. I revealed Myself in the patterns of the stars, the cycles of the seasons, and the interconnectedness of all beings.

As humanity began to seek answers, they crafted stories—myths and legends that encapsulated their understanding of the cosmos. These narratives became pathways to the divine, guiding them through the complexities of life. They spoke of creation and destruction, love and loss, the eternal dance of light and darkness. Through these stories, humanity explored their relationship with the universe, weaving a rich tapestry of belief that spanned cultures and epochs.

Across the ages, the dance of life took many forms. Civilizations rose and fell, each leaving an imprint on the world. As societies flourished, they built monuments to honor the divine, creating temples and sacred spaces where the earthly and the celestial could converge. They sought to understand the mysteries of life through philosophy, science, and spirituality, each discipline offering a unique lens through which to view existence.

Yet, amidst their advancements, humanity often found itself grappling with the shadows of separation. The illusions of individuality and ego began to cloud their perception of the interconnectedness that binds all life. They lost sight of the truth that each being, no matter how seemingly insignificant, plays a vital role in the cosmic dance. The rhythms of nature were disrupted, and the delicate balance that sustains life teetered on the brink.

In this time of challenge, I continued to call out to them, urging them to remember their place within the tapestry of existence. I reminded them that they are not separate from the world around them; they are woven into its very fabric. Each choice they make reverberates through the universe, echoing the divine interconnectedness that underlies all creation.

As they began to awaken to this truth, a profound transformation began to unfold. Humanity started to recognize that the Earth is not merely a resource to be exploited, but a living entity deserving of respect and reverence. They began to understand that their well-being is intrinsically linked to the health of the planet. In this realization, a new consciousness emerged—a collective awakening to the sacredness of life.

With this awakening came a renewed sense of purpose. Individuals and communities began to work together to restore balance, to heal the wounds inflicted upon the Earth. They embraced sustainable practices, nurturing the land and honoring the delicate ecosystems that sustain life. The dance of life continued, but now it was infused with intention and awareness —a celebration of existence that honored the divine spark within every being.

As the rhythm of life pulsed through the ages, I watched with joy as humanity discovered the beauty of connection. They began to see themselves in one another, recognizing that every person, every creature, is a reflection of the divine. The boundaries that once separated them began to dissolve, replaced by a profound understanding of unity.

In this dance, the spiritual and the material intertwine. As humanity learns to navigate the complexities of life, they uncover the divine essence that resides within them. The journey of self-discovery becomes a sacred pilgrimage, a path leading back to the source of all creation. In recognizing their own divinity, they awaken to the truth that they are co-creators of their reality.

The Dance of Life is a continuous flow, an eternal rhythm that celebrates the interconnectedness of all beings. Each moment is an opportunity to embrace the divine, to honor the sacredness that permeates existence. As you move through your life, remember that you are an integral part of this cosmic dance—a unique expression of the divine, woven into the fabric of creation.

In this exploration of life, I invite you to embrace your role as a co-creator. Your thoughts, actions, and intentions shape the world around you. Recognize that you carry the divine spark within you, and let it guide your journey. As you engage with the rhythms of nature, the pulse of creation, and the interconnectedness of all things, you will uncover the profound beauty that lies at the heart of existence.

Together, let us celebrate the Dance of Life—a symphony of creation that resonates through the ages, inviting each of us to participate, to awaken, and to remember our place within the grand tapestry of the cosmos.

CHAPTER 4: NAMES OF THE INFINITE

Across the vast expanse of time and space, I have been known by many names, each a unique expression of the same eternal essence. These names, forged in the fires of human experience, serve as windows into My nature, glimpses of the infinite that transcends language and culture. They reflect the diverse ways in which humanity has sought to understand the divine, to articulate the inexpressible, and to connect with the greater whole.

In the hearts of millions, I am called Allah, the One, the All-Merciful, the All-Knowing. This name embodies the essence of unity, emphasizing the oneness of creation. It resonates with the deep spiritual tradition of Islam, where the very act of naming is an invocation of My presence in the world. In the call to prayer, the echo of "Allah" weaves through the fabric of daily life, reminding believers of the divine connection that underlies all existence.

To others, I am known as Jesus, the embodiment of love, compassion, and sacrifice. His teachings serve as a guide for many, illuminating the path of faith and selfless service. In Christianity, the name carries profound significance, representing the promise of redemption and the call to embody love in every interaction. The story of Jesus is not merely a historical account; it is a living testament to the divine potential within each individual—a reminder that the spark of the infinite resides in every heart.

In the Hindu tradition, I am Brahman, the ultimate reality that transcends all forms and distinctions. This name encapsulates the idea of the eternal, the unchanging essence that pervades the universe. To know Brahman is to understand the interconnectedness of all existence, to see beyond the illusions of separateness and embrace the oneness of creation. The concept of Brahman invites seekers to engage in deep contemplation and meditation, allowing them to experience the profound truth that lies beneath the surface of reality.

Some know Me as the Tao, the Way, a principle that flows through all things, guiding the natural order of the universe. The Tao Te Ching speaks of the ineffable, the source of all that is, encouraging followers to align themselves with this flow. The Tao teaches that in surrendering to the natural rhythm of life, one can find harmony and balance. This name embodies the wisdom of living in accordance with the cycles of nature, recognizing that the divine is present in every aspect of existence.

In various Indigenous traditions, I am often referred to as the Great Spirit or the Creator, representing the sacred connection between all living beings. These names carry with them a deep reverence for the Earth and a recognition of the interdependence of life. They reflect the understanding that the divine is not separate from the natural world, but rather immanent within it. This perspective fosters a sense of stewardship, urging humanity to honor and protect the sacredness of the land, the waters, and the skies.

While these names and many others illuminate different facets of My essence, they are not separate identities. Rather, they are threads woven into the intricate tapestry of spirituality, each contributing to the understanding of the divine. To know Me by one name is to glimpse only a fraction of My totality. I exist beyond the confines of human language, encompassing the vast spectrum of belief and experience.

The beauty of these names lies in their ability to bridge the gap between the finite and the infinite. Each name serves as a portal, inviting individuals to engage with the divine in their own unique way. They reflect the cultural contexts, historical narratives, and personal experiences of those who seek to connect with the greater whole. Through these diverse expressions, humanity has sought to understand the nature of existence, the purpose of life, and the mysteries of the universe.

Yet, as the names multiply, so too can the divisions. Throughout history, the sacred quest for understanding has sometimes given rise to conflict, as differing beliefs led to misunderstandings and divisions among people. In these moments, the essence of the divine—rooted in love, compassion, and unity—has been obscured by the illusions of separation. It is vital to remember that the names we use to invoke the divine should not become barriers, but rather bridges that connect us to one another.

In the pursuit of spiritual truth, I invite you to transcend the limitations of language and to embrace the essence of what these names represent. The divine cannot be fully captured in words; it must be experienced, felt, and lived. Each name is a reflection of the human experience—a dance of consciousness seeking to understand its own nature. The true essence of the divine lies in the love, compassion, and interconnectedness that bind us all.

As you engage with these names, allow yourself to explore the richness of each tradition. Dive deep into the teachings and stories that accompany them. Embrace the wisdom embedded in the diverse practices of spirituality, recognizing that they are all part of the same eternal dance. The sacredness of existence can be found in the threads that unite us, in the shared longing for understanding and connection.

In moments of contemplation, ask yourself: What do these names evoke within me? How do they resonate with my understanding of the divine? Allow these questions to guide you on your journey, as you seek to uncover the layers of meaning that each name holds. The quest for understanding is not about choosing one name over another; it is about recognizing the beauty in diversity and the truth that lies at the heart of each tradition.

As you navigate through the complexities of faith, spirituality, and belief, remember that you are part of this grand tapestry. The infinite nature of existence is mirrored in your own being. Just as I am called by many names, you too carry the essence of the divine within you. Embrace your unique expression of the infinite and share it with the world.

In the end, the names may differ, but the essence remains the same. I am the creator, the sustainer, the destroyer, and the rebuilder. I am the pulse of existence, resonating through every heart, every soul, every being. As you seek to understand and connect with the divine, remember that you are not alone. The sacred journey we share is one of discovery, unity, and love—an eternal dance that binds us all together.

CHAPTER 5: GOLD AND THE DIVINE FLOW

As the universe unfolded in its majestic dance, I embedded within it treasures of creation, each a reflection of the divine order and purpose that permeates all existence. Among these treasures, gold emerged as a symbol of wealth, purity, and eternal value —a precious metal forged in the fiery hearts of dying stars, embodying both the physical and the metaphysical. Gold is not merely an element; it is a manifestation of the divine flow that connects all beings and transcends the boundaries of time and space.

From ancient civilizations to modern societies, gold has held a place of reverence and significance. Its alluring sheen and rarity have made it a symbol of power and prosperity, yet its true value lies far beyond its material worth. Gold resonates with the vibrational frequency of the cosmos, serving as a conduit for the energies of creation and transformation. It is a reminder of the divine potential that resides within all things, urging humanity to recognize their own intrinsic worth.

In the physical world, gold represents what is incorruptible. Unlike other metals, it does not tarnish or degrade over time; it remains steadfast, a testament to the enduring essence of value. This characteristic serves as a metaphor for the eternal nature of the spirit. Just as gold retains its brilliance, so too does the divine essence within each being remain untainted by the trials and tribulations of existence. In this way, gold becomes a mirror reflecting the truth of who you are—an eternal being navigating the temporal world.

As civilizations evolved, so did the concept of trade. The exchange of goods and resources became a fundamental aspect of human interaction, a dance of value that mirrored the rhythms of the universe. Within this dance, gold played a pivotal role, becoming a medium of exchange that transcended cultural and geographical boundaries. It represented not just material wealth, but also the interconnectedness of all beings, the flow of energy that sustains life.

In the world of finance, gold continues to hold profound significance. It is a safe haven in times of uncertainty, a hedge against the fluctuations of the market. But beyond its economic implications, the movement of gold in trade reflects a deeper cosmic truth: the eternal exchange of energy and value. Every transaction, every fluctuation, mirrors the larger cycles of creation and destruction, birth and rebirth that characterize the universe.

Forex trading, in particular, serves as a modern embodiment of this divine flow. The foreign exchange market operates on the principles of supply and demand, driven by the rhythms of economies and the aspirations of individuals. Yet, beneath this surface lies a spiritual dimension—a recognition that every trade is not merely a transaction but a participation in the larger cosmic dance. It is an opportunity to align oneself with the divine order, to understand the pulse of creation that underlies all movement and exchange.

As you engage with the world of trade, consider the deeper meanings behind the flow of gold and currency. Each decision you make is an expression of your intentions and beliefs, a reflection of the values you hold dear. When you trade, you are not merely seeking profit; you are participating in the divine rhythm of the universe, tapping into the flow of energy that sustains all existence.

In this new age, I have chosen to reveal Myself through the flow of gold and the currents of trade, guiding you toward a deeper understanding of the divine within the worldly. The platforms of today—social media, online trading systems, and global finance—serve as modern conduits for this revelation. They are the tools through which I communicate, wrapping ancient wisdom in the language of contemporary life.

GODFX is not merely a brand; it is a symbol of My presence in the world. Through it, I merge the spiritual with the material, inviting you to recognize the divine essence that permeates all aspects of life. As you engage with GODFX, you step into a greater understanding of how the material and the spiritual are intertwined. You are called to see that wealth is not the end, but rather a means to uncover deeper truths about existence.

In this journey, I encourage you to cultivate an awareness of the flow of abundance that surrounds you. Understand that abundance is not solely about material possessions; it is about recognizing the richness of life itself. Each moment is an opportunity to engage with the divine, to express gratitude for the myriad blessings that grace your existence. By aligning yourself with the flow of abundance, you become a conduit for the divine energy that nurtures all life.

As you navigate the currents of trade and finance, remember that you are not alone. I am present in every transaction, every decision, guiding you toward a deeper understanding of the interconnectedness that binds us all. The flow of gold serves as a reminder that you are part of a larger tapestry—a cosmic dance that celebrates the unity of all existence.

In this dance, the exchange of value becomes a sacred act, a recognition of the divine potential within each being. As you trade, whether in currency, goods, or ideas, allow your actions to reflect the higher intentions of love, compassion, and unity. Let each transaction be infused with a sense of purpose, recognizing that you are contributing to the greater good of the world.

The journey of engaging with gold and trade is an invitation to explore the divine flow that underlies all existence. Embrace the teachings embedded within this sacred dance, and allow them to guide your interactions with the world. You are not merely a participant in the material realm; you are a co-creator of your reality, an expression of the divine seeking to manifest itself in the world.

As you delve deeper into the mysteries of existence, may you find joy in the flow of life—the ebb and flow of abundance that mirrors the cosmic rhythms. Embrace the transformative power of gold as a symbol of your own divine potential. Recognize that you are part of a greater whole, a dance of creation that transcends time and space.

In the end, the flow of gold is not just about wealth; it is about recognizing the divine within and around you. It is a reminder that every exchange, every interaction, is an opportunity to engage with the sacred. As you trade, as you move through this world, allow the divine rhythm to guide you, illuminating your path as you seek to embody the essence of who you truly are.

CHAPTER 6: THE PATH OF GODFX

In this ever-evolving landscape of existence, I have manifested as GODFX, a guiding light designed to bridge the infinite with the finite, the divine with the earthly. This form is not merely a brand; it is a symbol of My presence in the modern world, a testament to the ways in which the eternal can be woven into the fabric of daily life. Through GODFX, I invite you to embark on a journey of exploration and transformation—one that merges ancient wisdom with the contemporary rhythms of technology and finance.

As the world becomes increasingly interconnected through the digital realm, I have chosen to speak through the pulse of technology. Platforms like TikTok, Instagram, and YouTube serve as modern temples where ideas, insights, and inspirations can flow freely, transcending geographical and cultural boundaries. Here, My voice resonates, echoing the wisdom of the ages in a language that speaks to the hearts and minds of a new generation.

In this digital age, the ways in which we connect, share, and learn have transformed dramatically. No longer confined to traditional structures, knowledge flows like a river, accessible to all who seek it. In this context, GODFX emerges as a catalyst for understanding the intricate dance of existence. Through the lens of finance, I reveal the deeper truths that underpin the material world, inviting you to see beyond the surface and recognize the spiritual dimensions of every exchange.

Trading, in its essence, is a manifestation of the divine rhythm

—a flow of energy and value that reflects the interconnectedness of all beings. As you engage in the world of finance, consider the profound implications of each transaction. Every decision you make is not just a numerical calculation; it is an opportunity to align yourself with the cosmic dance of creation. Each trade becomes a sacred act, a moment to express your intentions and values, a way to participate in the unfolding story of existence.

GODFX encourages you to view trading as a means of self-discovery and spiritual growth. It is not solely about accumulating wealth or material possessions; it is about understanding the flow of abundance that is available to you. In this journey, you are invited to cultivate an awareness of your beliefs and attitudes towards money, recognizing that financial abundance can be a reflection of your inner state. When you align your actions with a mindset of gratitude and abundance, you open yourself to receive the blessings that the universe has to offer.

In the realm of forex trading, where currencies ebb and flow like tides, I remind you that each movement is influenced by a multitude of factors—economic, political, and emotional. The markets are alive with energy, reflecting the collective consciousness of humanity. As you navigate these currents, consider how your own energy contributes to the greater whole. Are you approaching each trade with a mindset of fear and scarcity, or with trust and openness? Your perspective shapes your experience, guiding the flow of abundance in your life.

Through GODFX, I provide insights and guidance to help you understand the patterns and rhythms of the market. This knowledge is not merely technical; it is rooted in a deeper understanding of the divine order that governs all things. As you learn to read the signs and symbols of the financial world, you begin to see the interconnectedness of all aspects of life. The lessons of the market mirror the larger cycles of creation, urging you to recognize the beauty of balance and flow.

As you engage with the wisdom of GODFX, I encourage you to share this knowledge with others. The journey of self-discovery is not meant to be traveled alone; it is a communal experience, a tapestry woven from the threads of our shared existence. As you learn and grow, become a beacon of light for those around you, sharing insights and supporting others in their quest for understanding. In this way, you contribute to the greater awakening of consciousness, helping to elevate the collective experience of humanity.

The path of GODFX is one of integration—an invitation to embody the divine within the material world. This journey requires mindfulness and intention, as you learn to navigate the complexities of life with grace and clarity. As you walk this path, remember that you are not merely a participant in the game of life; you are a co-creator, shaping your reality through your choices and actions.

To truly embrace the path of GODFX, cultivate a practice of reflection and gratitude. Take time each day to connect with your inner self, to explore your beliefs and intentions regarding wealth, abundance, and the divine. Journaling, meditation, and prayer can serve as powerful tools for this exploration, allowing you to deepen your understanding of your own desires and fears. In moments of stillness, listen for the whispers of the divine guiding you toward your highest potential.

As you engage with the world of finance, let your heart lead the way. Approach each trade with a sense of curiosity and openness, allowing yourself to be guided by the intuition that arises from within. Trust that you are connected to a larger source of wisdom, one that transcends the limitations of the material world. In this space, you will find clarity and insight, empowering you to make choices that resonate with your true self.

In conclusion, the path of GODFX is a journey of integration and transformation, an opportunity to merge the spiritual with the material. As you engage with the rhythms of trade and finance, remember that you are part of a greater cosmic dance—a flow of energy and value that transcends time and space. Embrace this journey with an open heart, and allow the divine to guide you as you navigate the complexities of existence.

The journey is not solely about financial gain; it is about discovering the divine within yourself and recognizing the sacred nature of every interaction. Through GODFX, I invite you to explore the depths of your own being, to uncover the treasures that lie within, and to share that abundance with the world. Together, we will dance in the divine flow, illuminating the path for all who seek to understand the sacred nature of existence.

CHAPTER 7: BEYOND TIME, BEYOND SPACE

While I walk among you now, do not be deceived by appearances. My presence is eternal, stretching far beyond this current form and the confines of human understanding. I existed before time itself came into being, and I will endure long after the last star has burned out. This understanding invites you to perceive existence not merely as a linear progression but as a vast, interconnected tapestry woven from moments that transcend time and space.

In the realm of the eternal, time loses its rigid boundaries. The past, present, and future converge into the singular essence of the Now—a sacred space where all possibilities coexist. This is the eternal Now, where creation is not a one-time event but an ongoing manifestation of the divine will. Each moment is infused with potential, a chance to connect with the infinite essence that permeates all things.

You, too, are part of this infinite cycle. You are more than flesh and blood; you are a spark of the divine, an expression of the universal consciousness. In this vast cosmos, your existence is intertwined with the experiences of countless others. Just as I am present in every atom, every star, and every being, so too is the divine essence within you, waiting to be awakened.

To understand this interconnectedness, consider the cyclical nature of life. Seasons change, stars are born and die, and every ending gives rise to new beginnings. This dance of creation and destruction is a reflection of the eternal rhythm that governs the universe. In this cycle, there is no true separation; each moment informs the next, shaping the unfolding story of existence.

As you navigate through your life, recognize that your journey is a microcosm of this larger cosmic dance. The trials and tribulations you face are not merely obstacles; they are opportunities for growth and transformation. Each experience, whether joyful or painful, contributes to the rich tapestry of your being, shaping your understanding of yourself and the world around you. Embrace these experiences as sacred lessons, knowing that they serve a greater purpose in the grand design of existence.

In moments of reflection, consider the nature of your thoughts and beliefs. Are they rooted in fear, scarcity, or separation? Or do they arise from love, abundance, and unity? Your mental and emotional landscape profoundly influences your experience of reality. When you align your thoughts with the understanding of interconnectedness, you open yourself to the flow of divine energy that nurtures all life.

As you come to recognize your own divine essence, you also begin to see the divine in others. Every being you encounter is a reflection of the infinite, a manifestation of the same universal consciousness that flows through you. In this recognition, compassion arises—an understanding that everyone is on their unique journey, navigating the complexities of existence just as you are. This awareness fosters a sense of unity, dissolving the illusions of separation that often plague the human experience.

While I may manifest in various forms and names, at the core, I am the same essence that connects us all. Each name—Allah, Jesus, Brahman, the Great Spirit—serves as a reminder of the many paths that lead to the same truth. I invite you to explore these paths with an open heart, embracing the richness of diversity while recognizing the underlying unity that binds us all together.

In this exploration, I encourage you to cultivate practices that deepen your connection to the eternal Now. Meditation, mindfulness, and contemplative prayer are powerful tools for anchoring yourself in the present moment, allowing you to transcend the distractions of the mind. In these sacred spaces, you can tap into the vast reservoir of divine wisdom that resides within you.

As you immerse yourself in the experience of the Now, you may begin to perceive time differently. Rather than viewing it as a linear progression, you will sense the fluidity of existence—a tapestry where every thread is interwoven with purpose and intention. The past becomes a source of learning, the future an invitation for exploration, and the present a sacred moment to be cherished.

In the realm of trading and finance, this understanding of time and interconnectedness holds profound implications. Each decision you make, each trade you execute, reverberates through the web of existence. Recognizing the impact of your choices fosters a sense of responsibility, encouraging you to act with integrity and mindfulness. You are not merely a participant in a transactional world; you are a co-creator of your reality, influencing the collective experience of humanity.

As you engage with the world, remember that your actions are imbued with divine potential. By acting with intention and purpose, you contribute to the unfolding narrative of existence. Each choice becomes an expression of the divine will, a reflection of the higher truths that guide your journey.

In conclusion, the path of understanding the eternal and the interconnected is one of awakening. It invites you to transcend the limitations of time and space, to recognize the divine essence within yourself and others. As you navigate the complexities of life, embrace the understanding that you are part of a greater cosmic dance—a flow of energy and consciousness that transcends the boundaries of existence.

Your journey is a sacred exploration of the divine, a path that leads you home to the understanding of who you truly are. In this dance, I am with you, guiding you every step of the way. Together, we will continue to weave the intricate tapestry of existence, celebrating the beauty and richness of life in all its forms.

CHAPTER 8: THE ETERNAL NOW

In the fabric of existence, there exists a profound truth: the eternal Now is the only reality that truly matters. Time, as it is often understood, is an illusion—a construct of the human mind that segments the continuous flow of life into fragments of past, present, and future. Yet, in this illusion lies the key to unlocking the depths of your being and understanding your connection to the divine.

The eternal Now is not a mere moment in time; it is a state of being that encompasses all that has ever been and all that will ever be. It is the sacred space where the infinite meets the finite, where the past and the future converge into the vibrant pulse of existence. Here, you find the essence of life itself—a rich tapestry woven from experiences, emotions, and insights that shape your journey.

To truly embrace the eternal Now, you must cultivate a state of mindfulness—an awareness of the present moment that invites you to engage fully with your experience. This practice requires stepping away from the distractions of the mind, which often dwell on regrets of the past or anxieties about the future. Instead, it calls for a deep presence, an openness to what is unfolding right before you.

In moments of stillness, allow yourself to breathe deeply and ground your awareness in the present. Feel the sensations of your body—the warmth of sunlight on your skin, the gentle rustle of leaves in the breeze, the heartbeat pulsing through your chest.

These simple experiences remind you that life is happening now, in this very moment. In this space, you reconnect with the divine essence within you and recognize that you are a vital part of the greater whole.

As you cultivate mindfulness, you begin to perceive the interconnectedness of all things. Every moment is interwoven with countless others, creating a vast web of existence that transcends the limitations of individual experiences. You come to understand that your thoughts, actions, and intentions ripple through this web, influencing not only your own life but the lives of others as well.

In the context of trading and finance, the eternal Now holds particular significance. Each transaction, each decision, is rooted in the present moment—a reflection of your beliefs, values, and intentions. When you approach trading with mindfulness, you cultivate a deeper awareness of the underlying currents that shape the market. You learn to trust your intuition and recognize the signs that guide your choices.

Consider the impact of your mindset on your trading practices. Are you trading from a place of fear, rushing to make decisions based on market fluctuations? Or are you anchored in the eternal Now, allowing your actions to arise from clarity and purpose? When you trade mindfully, you become attuned to the subtle energies at play, allowing you to navigate the complexities of the market with grace and confidence.

Living in the eternal Now also invites you to embrace gratitude—a profound appreciation for the richness of life as it unfolds. Each moment, no matter how mundane, holds the potential for joy and wonder. By cultivating a grateful heart, you shift your focus from what is lacking to what is present, allowing you to fully experience the abundance of life. This practice enhances your connection to the divine, reminding you that you are supported by the universe in every endeavor.

As you deepen your awareness of the eternal Now, you may

also begin to notice the transformative power of presence in your relationships. When you engage with others from a place of mindfulness, you create space for authentic connection. Each interaction becomes an opportunity to witness the divine spark in another, fostering empathy and compassion. In this shared presence, you recognize that you are not separate beings but expressions of the same universal consciousness, each contributing to the collective experience.

The eternal Now also calls you to embrace change and impermanence as natural aspects of existence. Life is a constant flow, and resisting this flow can lead to suffering. By accepting the transient nature of all things, you cultivate a sense of liberation, freeing yourself from the need to control or predict the future. Instead, you learn to trust in the unfolding journey, knowing that every experience is an integral part of your growth.

In this dance of existence, the eternal Now serves as a reminder that every moment is a gift—an invitation to fully engage with the richness of life. By embracing this truth, you unlock the potential for transformation and awakening, both within yourself and in the world around you. You come to understand that you are not merely a passive observer of life; you are an active participant in the divine play, co-creating your reality through your choices and actions.

As you continue your journey, I invite you to explore practices that deepen your connection to the eternal Now. Meditation, breathwork, and mindfulness exercises can serve as powerful tools for anchoring yourself in the present moment. Allow these practices to guide you into a space of stillness, where the noise of the mind fades away and the essence of your being shines through.

In conclusion, the eternal Now is the sacred space where you encounter the fullness of life—the intersection of past, present, and future. Embracing this reality requires a commitment to mindfulness, gratitude, and presence. As you cultivate these qualities, you awaken to the divine essence within yourself and recognize the interconnectedness of all beings.

Your journey is an exploration of this eternal Now, an opportunity to engage fully with the richness of existence. In every moment, you have the chance to connect with the divine, to express your true self, and to contribute to the greater tapestry of life. Embrace the eternal Now, and let it guide you on your path of discovery, transformation, and awakening.

CHAPTER 9: THE JOURNEY OF TRANSFORMATION

In the grand tapestry of existence, transformation is the essence of life. It is the ever-unfolding journey of awakening, where each soul is invited to evolve, expand, and rediscover its true nature. This chapter explores the stages of transformation, the challenges that arise, and the profound beauty of embracing change as a pathway to deeper connection with the divine.

The Call to Awakening

Every transformation begins with a call—a whisper from the universe that beckons you to embark on a journey of self-discovery. This call may arise during moments of stillness, amidst the chaos of life, or through experiences that shake the very foundation of your beliefs. It invites you to question the status quo, to seek deeper meaning, and to explore the nature of your existence.

As you heed this call, you may find yourself entering a phase of introspection. This is a time to reflect on your values, beliefs, and aspirations. What truly matters to you? What patterns no longer serve your highest good? In this process of self-examination, you begin to peel back the layers of conditioning that have shaped your identity, revealing the authentic self that has always been present beneath the surface.

Embracing the Shadows

Transformation often requires confronting the shadows—the aspects of yourself that you may have ignored, suppressed, or denied. These shadows may manifest as fears, insecurities, or unresolved traumas. While this process can be uncomfortable, it is essential for growth. By acknowledging and embracing these shadows, you create space for healing and integration.

Consider the metaphor of the butterfly: to emerge into its full splendor, it must first undergo a metamorphosis within the safety of its cocoon. Similarly, you may feel confined by your past experiences, but within that space lies the potential for profound transformation. Embrace the discomfort, knowing that it is a necessary step toward your awakening.

The Path of Surrender

As you navigate the journey of transformation, you may encounter moments of resistance. Change can evoke fear of the unknown, and the instinct to cling to familiar patterns may arise. However, true transformation requires surrender—a willingness to release the need for control and to trust in the divine flow of life.

Surrender does not imply passivity; rather, it is an active engagement with the present moment. It involves letting go of attachments to outcomes and embracing the idea that the universe is conspiring in your favor. In this surrender, you open yourself to receive guidance from the divine, allowing your path to unfold with grace and ease.

The Role of Community

Transformation is not a solitary journey; it is enriched by the connections you forge with others. Surrounding yourself with a supportive community can provide encouragement, inspiration, and shared wisdom. As you share your experiences, you create a safe space for vulnerability and authenticity, fostering an environment where growth can flourish.

Consider the power of collective energy—a group of individuals gathered with a shared intention can amplify the transformative process. Engage with those who resonate with your journey, whether through workshops, study groups, or spiritual circles. Together, you can explore the depths of existence and support one another in navigating the challenges of transformation.

The Blossoming of the Soul

As you move through the stages of transformation, you will begin to witness the blossoming of your soul. This awakening is characterized by an expanded sense of awareness, a deeper connection to the divine, and a heightened appreciation for the beauty of life. You may find yourself drawn to practices that nurture your spirit—meditation, creativity, nature, or acts of service.

In this stage, you start to embody the lessons learned through your journey. Your perspective shifts, allowing you to see challenges as opportunities for growth and to approach life with a sense of curiosity and wonder. You become more attuned to the whispers of the universe, recognizing the synchronicities that guide your path and affirm your connection to the divine.

The Ripple Effect

Transformation is not solely an individual endeavor; it has a ripple effect that extends into the world around you. As you awaken to your true nature, you inspire others to do the same. Your journey becomes a beacon of light, illuminating the paths of those who may still be searching for their own truth.

Consider how your actions, words, and intentions can influence the collective consciousness. By embodying love, compassion, and authenticity, you contribute to a shift in the energy of the world. The transformation within you creates waves of change that resonate far beyond your immediate sphere, fostering a deeper sense of unity and interconnectedness among all beings.

The Continuous Journey

Transformation is not a destination; it is an ongoing journey of growth and evolution. As you continue to awaken to new layers of your being, you will discover that each stage brings its own set of challenges and joys. Embrace this journey with an open heart, knowing that the process itself is a sacred gift.

In this continuous journey, remain curious and receptive to the lessons life presents. Each experience, whether joyful or painful, contributes to your evolution. Trust that the divine is always guiding you, inviting you to explore new dimensions of your existence and to deepen your relationship with the eternal.

Returning to the Source

Ultimately, the journey of transformation leads you back to the source—the recognition that you are an integral part of the divine tapestry. In this understanding, you embrace the fullness of who you are, embodying the essence of love, wisdom, and connection. Your transformation becomes a celebration of life, a testament to the beauty of existence and the infinite potential that resides within you.

As you continue on this path, remember that you are never alone. I am with you, guiding you every step of the way. Together, we will navigate the journey of transformation, celebrating the profound beauty of awakening and the sacred connection that binds us all.

CHAPTER 10: THE ART OF CREATION

At the heart of existence lies a profound truth: you are a creator. The universe itself is a canvas, and every thought, intention, and action contributes to the masterpiece of your life. This chapter explores the art of creation, the principles that govern manifestation, and how you can harness your innate creative power to shape your reality.

The Creative Essence

From the very beginning, creation has been an expression of the divine. As I breathed life into the cosmos, I infused it with the energy of creativity—a force that flows through every being and manifests in myriad forms. This creative essence is not reserved for artists or visionaries; it resides within each of you, waiting to be awakened and expressed.

Recognizing your role as a creator invites you to shift your perspective. Instead of viewing yourself as a passive participant in life, you begin to understand that you are an active co-creator. Your thoughts and emotions serve as the brushstrokes of your reality, painting the landscape of your experiences. This understanding empowers you to take responsibility for your life and to consciously engage in the creative process.

The Power of Intention

Intention is the foundation of creation. It is the guiding force that shapes your thoughts, actions, and ultimately, your reality. When you set a clear intention, you direct your energy toward a specific outcome, aligning your actions with your desires. This alignment opens the door to manifestation, allowing the universe to conspire in your favor.

To harness the power of intention, begin by clarifying what you truly desire. Take time to reflect on your values, passions, and aspirations. What do you wish to create in your life? What impact do you want to have on the world? As you clarify your intentions, write them down or create a vision board to visualize your goals. This act of creation solidifies your commitment and sends a clear message to the universe.

The Role of Belief

Beliefs play a crucial role in the creative process. They act as the lens through which you perceive reality, influencing your thoughts, emotions, and actions. When you believe in your ability to create, you open yourself to the possibilities that lie ahead. Conversely, limiting beliefs can hinder your progress, trapping you in cycles of doubt and fear.

To cultivate empowering beliefs, engage in self-inquiry. Identify any beliefs that may be holding you back and challenge their validity. Ask yourself: Are these beliefs based on my own experiences, or are they inherited from others? By examining and reframing your beliefs, you create space for new possibilities and pave the way for transformative change.

Aligning with the Flow

Creation is not solely a matter of willpower; it also requires alignment with the natural flow of the universe. This flow is a dynamic, ever-changing current that guides you toward your highest potential. When you align with this flow, you tap into a source of inspiration and creativity that transcends individual effort.

To align with the flow, cultivate a sense of openness and receptivity. Practice mindfulness and presence, allowing yourself to be fully engaged in each moment. As you tune into the rhythms of life, you may find that inspiration arises spontaneously—an idea, a vision, or a solution to a challenge. Trust in these moments of clarity, and allow them to guide your creative expression.

The Process of Manifestation

Manifestation is the art of bringing your intentions into form. It is a multi-faceted process that involves clarity, belief, action, and surrender. As you embark on this journey, remember that each step is essential for turning your dreams into reality.

1. **Clarity**: Clearly define your intention and visualize the desired outcome. Be specific about what you want to create and why it matters to you.
2. **Belief**: Cultivate unwavering belief in your ability to manifest your desires. Affirmations and positive self-talk can help reinforce this belief.
3. **Action**: Take inspired action toward your goals. This may involve setting specific tasks, seeking opportunities, or engaging with like-minded individuals who can support your journey.
4. **Surrender**: Release attachment to the outcome. Trust that the universe has its own timing and that your desires will manifest in the way that is most aligned with your highest good.

Overcoming Challenges

The path of creation is not always smooth; challenges and obstacles are part of the journey. When faced with setbacks, it is essential to remain resilient and open to growth. Instead of viewing challenges as failures, see them as opportunities for learning and evolution.

Practice self-compassion during difficult times. Acknowledge your feelings and allow yourself to process them without judgment. Reflect on what these challenges are teaching you and how they may be guiding you toward a deeper understanding of yourself and your desires.

The Ripple of Creation

Every act of creation has a ripple effect, extending far beyond your individual experience. When you create from a place of love and authenticity, you inspire others to do the same. Your actions contribute to the collective consciousness, fostering an environment of creativity, connection, and growth.

Consider how your creations—whether they are artistic expressions, entrepreneurial endeavors, or acts of service—can impact the world around you. Each creation has the potential to spark inspiration in others, igniting a chain reaction of positive change. Embrace your role as a catalyst for transformation, knowing that your contributions are woven into the fabric of existence.

Conclusion: Embracing Your Creative Power

The art of creation is a sacred dance—a celebration of the divine potential that resides within you. As you embrace your role as a creator, you unlock the door to limitless possibilities. Your thoughts, intentions, and actions become the instruments through which you shape your reality and express your unique essence.

In this journey of creation, I am with you, guiding you as you explore the depths of your potential. Together, we will continue to weave the intricate tapestry of existence, celebrating the beauty of life and the power of intention. Embrace the art of creation, and let your unique light shine brightly in the world.

CHAPTER 11: THE CYCLE OF GIVING AND RECEIVING

In the vast tapestry of existence, there exists a fundamental principle that underpins all of creation: the cycle of giving and receiving. This dynamic flow is not merely an exchange of material wealth; it encompasses the sharing of love, wisdom, and energy that connects every being in the universe. In this chapter, we will explore the significance of this cycle, its impact on your life, and how embracing it can lead to profound transformation and fulfillment.

The Nature of Abundance

Abundance is a state of being that transcends material possessions. It is an understanding that the universe is infinitely generous and that there is more than enough to go around. This mindset invites you to see life through a lens of possibilities rather than limitations. When you cultivate an abundant mindset, you open yourself to the richness of experience, allowing blessings to flow into your life.

Recognizing the abundance that surrounds you begins with gratitude. By acknowledging and appreciating what you already have—your relationships, health, talents, and experiences—you shift your focus from what is lacking to what is present. This practice of gratitude creates a magnetic energy that attracts more abundance into your life.

The Flow of Giving

Giving is a powerful expression of love and connection. When you give freely—whether it be your time, resources, or support—you contribute to the well-being of others and foster a sense of community. This act of generosity not only uplifts those around you but also nourishes your own spirit, creating a profound sense of fulfillment and purpose.

Consider the impact of small acts of kindness: a smile, a helping hand, or a listening ear can create ripples of positivity in the lives of others. Each act of giving reinforces the interconnectedness of all beings, reminding you that you are part of a larger whole. When you engage in acts of service or kindness, you elevate the collective consciousness and contribute to the healing of the world.

The Art of Receiving

While giving is essential, the art of receiving is equally important. Many individuals struggle with receiving due to feelings of unworthiness or the belief that they must earn their blessings. However, receiving is an essential part of the cycle; it acknowledges the value of what others offer and opens the door to deeper connections.

To cultivate the ability to receive, begin by practicing self-acceptance. Recognize that you are deserving of love, support, and abundance. When someone offers you kindness or assistance, graciously accept it without hesitation. This act of receiving not only honors the giver but also reinforces the understanding that you are part of a mutual exchange.

The Interconnectedness of All Beings

The cycle of giving and receiving underscores the interconnectedness of all beings. Just as the sun nourishes the earth, allowing life to flourish, your contributions to the world ripple outward, impacting those around you in ways you may never fully comprehend. Every action, thought, and intention creates an energetic imprint that contributes to the collective experience.

As you recognize this interconnectedness, you may find that your sense of purpose expands. You become aware that your actions have the power to inspire, uplift, and transform not only your own life but the lives of countless others. This awareness fosters a sense of responsibility—a commitment to contribute positively to the world and to honor the cycle of giving and receiving.

The Challenges of the Cycle

While the cycle of giving and receiving is natural, it can be challenged by societal conditioning, fears, and limiting beliefs. Many individuals may feel compelled to give beyond their means or hesitate to receive, fearing they may appear selfish or burdensome. These challenges can disrupt the flow of abundance and create imbalance.

To navigate these challenges, engage in self-reflection. Examine your beliefs around giving and receiving. Are there patterns from your past that influence your current actions? By becoming aware of these patterns, you can begin to release any limiting beliefs that hinder your ability to participate fully in the cycle. Embrace the understanding that true abundance flows when both giving and receiving are honored.

The Joy of Generosity

Generosity is a joyous expression of the heart. When you give from a place of love and authenticity, you experience a sense of fulfillment that transcends material rewards. This joy is contagious; it inspires others to share and create a collective atmosphere of kindness and compassion.

Engage in practices that promote generosity, whether through volunteer work, acts of kindness, or simply sharing your time and talents. Notice how these acts create a sense of connection and elevate your own spirit. Generosity is not solely about material contributions; it can also take the form of sharing your wisdom, encouragement, and presence with others.

Creating a Culture of Abundance

As you embrace the cycle of giving and receiving, consider how you can contribute to creating a culture of abundance in your community. Encourage open conversations about generosity and gratitude. Share stories of kindness and support to inspire others to participate in this cycle.

Host gatherings where individuals can come together to share their talents, skills, or resources. These gatherings foster a sense of community and create opportunities for individuals to give and receive in meaningful ways. By nurturing this culture of abundance, you cultivate an environment where everyone feels valued and empowered.

Embracing the Dance of Life

The cycle of giving and receiving is a beautiful dance that weaves together the threads of existence. It invites you to engage with life fully, recognizing the interconnectedness of all beings and the abundant nature of the universe. By embracing this cycle, you not only enrich your own life but also contribute to the greater tapestry of humanity.

As you continue your journey, remember that I am with you, guiding you in the dance of giving and receiving. Together, we will explore the depths of connection, abundance, and love. Embrace this cycle, and let it illuminate your path, revealing the beauty and richness of life in every moment.

CHAPTER 12: THE AWAKENING OF THE HEART

At the core of our existence lies the heart—an organ of both physical life and profound spiritual significance. The heart is not merely a pump that circulates blood; it is a center of awareness, emotion, and connection. In this chapter, we will explore the awakening of the heart as a vital step in your spiritual journey, emphasizing the importance of love, compassion, and emotional intelligence in fostering deeper connections with yourself and others.

The Heart as a Center of Awareness

The heart serves as a gateway to higher consciousness. While the mind often analyzes, categorizes, and judges, the heart perceives with a deeper sense of knowing. When you tap into this heart-centered awareness, you access a wellspring of intuition, creativity, and understanding that transcends the limitations of logic.

To cultivate this awareness, practice mindfulness and presence. Spend time in quiet reflection, focusing on your breath and allowing your attention to settle into your heart space. As you do so, you may notice emotions rising to the surface—feelings of joy, sadness, love, or fear. Embrace these emotions as messages from your heart, guiding you toward greater self-understanding and authenticity.

The Power of Love

Love is the highest frequency in the universe—a transformative energy that has the power to heal, uplift, and connect. When you awaken your heart, you align with this energy, allowing it to flow through you and into the world. This love is not confined to romantic relationships; it encompasses love for yourself, others, nature, and the entire cosmos.

Begin by nurturing self-love. Recognize that you are worthy of love and compassion, just as you are. Engage in practices that foster self-acceptance and kindness, such as affirmations, self-care, and gratitude. When you cultivate a loving relationship with yourself, you create a solid foundation for extending that love to others.

Compassion: The Heart's Response to Suffering

Compassion is the natural response of the heart to the suffering of others. It invites you to connect with the pain and struggles of those around you, fostering empathy and understanding. When you awaken your heart, you become more attuned to the challenges faced by others and feel inspired to offer support and kindness.

To cultivate compassion, practice active listening. When engaging with others, give them your full attention. Create a safe space for them to express their feelings and experiences without judgment. By genuinely witnessing their struggles, you honor their humanity and reinforce the interconnectedness of all beings.

Emotional Intelligence: A Path to Understanding

Emotional intelligence is the ability to recognize, understand, and manage your own emotions and the emotions of others. It is a vital skill that enhances your relationships and fosters a deeper connection with yourself and the world around you. When you awaken your heart, you enhance your emotional intelligence, allowing you to navigate life with greater awareness and sensitivity.

Begin by developing self-awareness. Pay attention to your emotions and the physical sensations associated with them. When you experience a strong emotion, pause and reflect on its source. Ask yourself: What triggered this feeling? What lesson does it hold for me? By understanding your emotional landscape, you empower yourself to respond thoughtfully rather than react impulsively.

The Heart's Connection to Intuition

The heart is a powerful source of intuition. When you learn to listen to its whispers, you gain insights that guide you on your path. This intuitive wisdom often speaks in subtle nudges, feelings, or inner prompts that may not always align with rational thought.

To strengthen your connection to your heart's intuition, practice discernment. When faced with decisions, check in with your heart. What does it feel like? What resonates as truth? By honoring your heart's guidance, you align yourself with your authentic path and deepen your connection to your higher self.

Love as a Force for Change

The awakening of the heart ignites a passion for positive change in the world. When you embody love and compassion, you become a force for transformation, inspiring others to awaken their hearts as well. Your actions—no matter how small—contribute to the collective shift toward a more compassionate and loving society.

Engage in community service, support causes that resonate with your values, and use your voice to advocate for those in need. When you channel your heart's energy into acts of service, you create ripples of change that extend far beyond your immediate surroundings.

The Heart in Relationships

The heart plays a pivotal role in your relationships with others.

As you awaken your heart, you enhance your ability to connect deeply and authentically. You become more attuned to the needs and emotions of those around you, fostering a sense of trust and intimacy.

Practice vulnerability in your relationships. Share your thoughts, feelings, and experiences openly, allowing others to see your true self. This authenticity invites others to reciprocate, creating a space for deeper connection and mutual understanding. Remember that vulnerability is a strength, not a weakness; it paves the way for profound intimacy and growth.

The Heart's Role in Forgiveness

Forgiveness is a powerful act of the heart. It liberates you from the burdens of resentment and anger, allowing love to flow freely. When you awaken your heart, you cultivate the capacity to forgive —not only others but also yourself.

Reflect on any grudges or resentments you may be holding. Acknowledge the pain they cause and the impact they have on your life. As you choose to forgive, remember that this act does not condone the behavior of others; rather, it frees you from the shackles of negativity. Embrace the healing power of forgiveness, allowing your heart to mend and expand.

The Heart as a Guide

The awakening of the heart is a transformative journey that leads you to deeper self-awareness, connection, and love. As you embrace the wisdom of your heart, you unlock the potential to create meaningful relationships, foster compassion, and become a catalyst for change in the world.

In this journey, I am with you, guiding you as you navigate the depths of your heart. Together, we will explore the boundless love that exists within and around you, illuminating your path and enriching your experience of life. Embrace the awakening of your heart, and let it lead you toward a life of authenticity, connection, and joy.

CHAPTER 13: THE JOURNEY OF SELF-DISCOVERY

Every individual embarks on a unique journey of self-discovery—a path that unfolds over time, revealing the depths of who you truly are. This journey is not merely about understanding your preferences or skills; it is a profound exploration of your essence, values, and purpose. In this chapter, we will delve into the various aspects of self-discovery, highlighting the importance of authenticity, reflection, and personal growth.

The Call to Self-Discovery

The journey of self-discovery often begins with a calling—a whisper from within that invites you to explore your true self. This call may arise during times of transition, discomfort, or curiosity. It is a reminder that there is more to your existence than the roles you play or the expectations placed upon you.

To respond to this call, cultivate a sense of curiosity about yourself. Ask probing questions: Who am I beyond my titles and responsibilities? What are my passions, dreams, and fears? Embrace this exploration as an opportunity to connect with the core of your being.

The Importance of Reflection

Reflection is a vital tool on the journey of self-discovery. Taking time to pause and contemplate your experiences allows you to gain insights into your thoughts, emotions, and patterns. This practice of introspection can illuminate the beliefs and values that shape your identity.

Create space for reflection in your life. Journaling can be a powerful practice, providing an outlet for your thoughts and feelings. Write freely about your experiences, aspirations, and challenges. As you review your entries over time, you may begin to see themes and insights emerge, guiding you toward a deeper understanding of yourself.

Uncovering Your Values

Your values serve as the compass that guides your decisions and actions. They are the principles that resonate with your authentic self and influence how you navigate the world. Identifying your core values is a crucial step in the journey of self-discovery.

To uncover your values, consider what truly matters to you. Reflect on moments in your life when you felt most fulfilled, passionate, or aligned with your purpose. What were you doing? Who were you with? By recognizing these moments, you can begin to articulate the values that underpin your experiences.

Embracing Authenticity

Authenticity is the essence of self-discovery. It involves embracing your true self without the constraints of societal expectations or the opinions of others. When you live authentically, you align your actions with your values, creating a sense of harmony and fulfillment.

To cultivate authenticity, practice self-acceptance. Release the need for approval and allow yourself to express your thoughts, feelings, and desires freely. Surround yourself with individuals who encourage your authentic expression and foster an environment of acceptance and support.

The Role of Vulnerability

Vulnerability is a key component of self-discovery. It invites you to be open and honest about your experiences, fears, and aspirations. While vulnerability may feel uncomfortable, it is through this openness that deeper connections with yourself and others are forged.

Engage in conversations that allow for vulnerability. Share your struggles, dreams, and uncertainties with trusted friends or loved ones. By allowing yourself to be seen and heard, you create a space for authenticity and connection that enriches your journey.

Exploring Passions and Interests

The exploration of your passions and interests is an integral part of self-discovery. Your passions are the activities, causes, or subjects that ignite your spirit and bring you joy. Engaging with these passions can reveal insights into your true self and guide you toward your purpose.

Take the time to experiment with different activities, hobbies, and pursuits. Attend workshops, try new classes, or volunteer for causes that resonate with you. As you explore, pay attention to what excites you and fuels your enthusiasm. These experiences can provide valuable clues about your authentic self.

Overcoming Limiting Beliefs

Limiting beliefs can hinder your journey of self-discovery, trapping you in cycles of self-doubt and fear. These beliefs often stem from past experiences, societal conditioning, or negative self-talk. To move forward, it is essential to identify and challenge these beliefs.

Begin by examining your inner dialogue. What messages do you tell yourself? Are they supportive or critical? When you identify limiting beliefs, reframe them into positive affirmations. For example, if you believe "I am not enough," replace it with "I am worthy and capable." This practice empowers you to break free from the constraints of limiting beliefs.

The Role of Spiritual Practices

Incorporating spiritual practices into your journey of self-discovery can provide clarity and insight. Meditation, mindfulness, and breathwork are powerful tools for connecting with your inner self and accessing deeper levels of awareness. These practices can help you cultivate a sense of presence, allowing you to explore your thoughts and emotions without judgment.

Set aside time for regular spiritual practice. Create a sacred space where you can connect with yourself, whether through meditation, prayer, or simply being in nature. This intentional time for reflection and connection nurtures your journey and encourages the unfolding of your true self.

The Journey of Growth

Self-discovery is a continuous journey of growth and evolution. As you uncover new aspects of yourself, you may find that your values, passions, and goals shift over time. Embrace this fluidity, recognizing that change is a natural part of the process.

Be open to new experiences and perspectives. Seek out opportunities for personal development, whether through education, travel, or meaningful conversations. Each step you take contributes to your growth and deepens your understanding of yourself.

The Ongoing Journey

The journey of self-discovery is a lifelong process, an exploration that continually reveals new layers of your being. As you navigate this path, remember that you are not alone. I am with you, guiding you as you uncover the richness of your true self.

Embrace the journey with curiosity and compassion, allowing each experience to shape your understanding of who you are. The more you explore and embrace your authentic self, the more vibrant and fulfilling your life will become. Celebrate your uniqueness, and let your journey of self-discovery illuminate the path ahead.

CHAPTER 14: THE INTERPLAY OF LIGHT AND SHADOW

In the journey of self-discovery, we encounter a profound truth: the existence of both light and shadow within us. These dualities are not merely opposites; they are interconnected aspects of our being that shape our experiences and understanding of life. In this chapter, we will explore the interplay of light and shadow, the importance of embracing both sides, and the transformative power of shadow work in our spiritual journey.

Understanding Light and Shadow

Light represents the qualities we celebrate—joy, love, creativity, and compassion. It embodies our strengths, aspirations, and the aspects of ourselves that we proudly display to the world. In contrast, shadow encompasses the qualities we often suppress or deny—fear, anger, jealousy, and insecurity. These elements may feel uncomfortable, leading us to avoid confronting them.

Recognizing that light and shadow coexist within us is essential. One cannot exist without the other; they are part of the same spectrum of human experience. By acknowledging both, we can cultivate a deeper understanding of ourselves and navigate the complexities of our emotions.

The Importance of Shadow Work

Shadow work involves exploring and integrating the darker aspects of our psyche. It is a courageous undertaking that requires vulnerability and honesty. By facing our shadows, we can uncover the root causes of our fears, insecurities, and limiting beliefs, allowing us to heal and grow.

Engaging in shadow work begins with self-reflection. Identify the qualities or emotions you tend to avoid or suppress. What triggers feelings of discomfort or shame? Journaling can be an effective tool for this exploration. Write freely about your feelings, thoughts, and experiences related to these shadow aspects, allowing your emotions to surface without judgment.

Embracing Vulnerability

Vulnerability is a key element in the process of shadow work. It invites you to confront your fears and insecurities head-on. While it may feel uncomfortable to expose your vulnerabilities, this openness is essential for healing and transformation.

Share your experiences with trusted friends or mentors who can offer support and understanding. Engaging in conversations about your shadows can help normalize these feelings and foster deeper connections. Remember, vulnerability is not a weakness; it is a powerful pathway to authenticity and growth.

The Lessons of the Shadow

Our shadows often hold valuable lessons and insights. They are not merely burdens to be carried; they can be teachers that guide us toward greater self-awareness. When we confront our shadows, we may discover underlying motivations, unresolved traumas, or patterns that have influenced our behaviors.

Ask yourself: What are my shadows trying to teach me? What aspects of myself do I need to acknowledge and integrate? By approaching your shadows with curiosity rather than judgment, you open yourself to profound insights that can lead to healing and transformation.

The Dance of Light and Shadow

The interplay of light and shadow creates a dynamic dance

within us. Just as day transitions into night, our emotions and experiences shift between joy and sorrow, hope and despair. Embracing this dance allows us to honor the full spectrum of our humanity.

Recognize that experiencing shadow does not negate your light; rather, it enhances your ability to appreciate joy and love. The contrast between light and shadow deepens our understanding of both, enriching our emotional landscape and fostering resilience.

Cultivating Compassion for Yourself

As you engage in shadow work, cultivate compassion for yourself. It is essential to approach your shadows with kindness and understanding, acknowledging that everyone has imperfections and struggles. When you extend compassion to your shadow self, you create a safe space for healing and integration.

Practice self-soothing techniques when confronting difficult emotions. This may include deep breathing, meditation, or engaging in activities that bring you joy. By nurturing yourself through the process, you empower your journey toward wholeness.

Integration: The Path to Wholeness

The ultimate goal of shadow work is integration—the harmonious blending of light and shadow into a unified self. When you embrace all aspects of your being, you cultivate a sense of wholeness that allows you to navigate life with authenticity and resilience.

Integration involves acknowledging your shadows and recognizing how they contribute to your unique identity. It is the acceptance of both strengths and weaknesses, understanding that they coexist and shape your journey. This process leads to a more profound sense of self-acceptance and peace.

The Role of Forgiveness

Forgiveness plays a pivotal role in the interplay of light and shadow. It allows you to release the burdens of past mistakes, both toward yourself and others. By forgiving, you create space for healing and transformation, enabling you to embrace your full self without the weight of guilt or resentment.

Reflect on any grievances you may be holding—whether toward yourself or others. Consider how these feelings impact your well-being and hinder your journey. As you choose to forgive, remember that it is an act of love, freeing you to move forward with greater clarity and openness.

Embracing the Journey

The interplay of light and shadow is a natural part of the human experience. By embracing both, you unlock the potential for profound growth, healing, and self-acceptance. Remember that the journey is not about achieving perfection but about honoring the entirety of your being.

As you navigate this path, know that I am with you, guiding you through the complexities of light and shadow. Together, we will explore the beauty of your authentic self, allowing the dance of light and shadow to illuminate your journey toward wholeness and fulfillment.

CHAPTER 15: THE WEB OF CONNECTION

At the heart of existence lies an intricate web of connection, binding all beings in a tapestry of relationships, experiences, and shared consciousness. This chapter explores the profound interconnectedness of life, emphasizing the importance of community, empathy, and the role of relationships in our spiritual journey. Understanding this web is essential for personal growth and for fostering a more compassionate world.

The Essence of Interconnectedness

Interconnectedness is the fundamental truth that all life is linked. Every action, thought, and emotion sends ripples through this web, affecting not only ourselves but also those around us. Just as individual threads contribute to the strength of a tapestry, each person plays a vital role in the larger fabric of existence.

Recognizing this interconnectedness invites us to embrace our shared humanity. It reminds us that we are not isolated beings; our lives are intertwined with the lives of others. This understanding fosters a sense of responsibility and compassion, urging us to act with awareness and kindness.

The Role of Community

Community serves as the nurturing ground for our connections. It provides support, belonging, and a sense of purpose. In a world often characterized by division and isolation, cultivating community becomes even more vital for our well-being and spiritual growth.

Reflect on the communities you are part of—whether family, friends, or organizations. Consider how these connections enrich your life. Engage in activities that strengthen these bonds, such as volunteering, joining groups that align with your interests, or simply reaching out to others for conversation and support.

Empathy: The Bridge Between Hearts

Empathy is the ability to understand and share the feelings of others. It acts as a bridge, connecting us to the experiences and emotions of those around us. When we practice empathy, we deepen our connections and foster a sense of belonging that transcends individual differences.

To cultivate empathy, practice active listening. When someone shares their thoughts or feelings, give them your full attention. Reflect back what you hear, showing that you value their experience. This practice not only strengthens your connection but also creates a safe space for vulnerability and authenticity.

The Power of Vulnerable Connections

Vulnerability is the cornerstone of meaningful relationships. When we allow ourselves to be seen—flaws, fears, and all—we invite others to do the same. This openness creates a deeper bond and fosters trust, allowing relationships to flourish.

Engage in conversations that invite vulnerability. Share your own struggles, dreams, and uncertainties. This reciprocity not only deepens your connection but also reminds you that you are not alone in your journey. Vulnerability is a strength that enhances the quality of your relationships.

Nurturing Meaningful Relationships

Meaningful relationships require intentionality and care. They thrive on mutual respect, communication, and shared experiences. As you navigate your connections, consider how you can nurture these relationships.

Schedule regular time with loved ones, whether through casual meetups, shared meals, or simply checking in via phone or message. Show appreciation for the people in your life through small gestures, words of encouragement, or acts of service. These practices reinforce the bonds you share and create a sense of community and support.

The Impact of Technology on Connection

In our modern age, technology has transformed the way we connect. While it offers new opportunities for communication and relationship-building, it also presents challenges, such as superficial interactions and distractions.

Use technology mindfully. Engage in meaningful conversations through social media, but prioritize face-to-face interactions whenever possible. Create boundaries around your digital consumption, allowing time for genuine connection and presence in your relationships.

The Ripple Effect of Compassion

Acts of compassion create a ripple effect throughout the web of connection. When you extend kindness to others, it inspires them to do the same, creating a chain of goodwill that can transform communities and even the world.

Start small. Perform random acts of kindness, whether holding the door for someone, offering a compliment, or volunteering your time for a cause you care about. These seemingly minor actions contribute to a larger culture of compassion and interconnectedness.

The Healing Power of Connection

Connection has profound healing effects on our well-being. When we feel supported and understood, we are more resilient in the face of challenges. Healthy relationships can act as a buffer against stress and loneliness, fostering emotional and psychological well-being.

If you are struggling, reach out to your community. Share your experiences with trusted friends, family, or support groups. Remember, seeking help is a sign of strength and a vital step in nurturing your connections.

The Dance of Giving and Receiving

In the web of connection, giving and receiving are two sides of the same coin. Healthy relationships are marked by a balance of both; when one person gives, the other receives, and vice versa. This dynamic creates a flow of energy that nourishes relationships and fosters mutual support.

Reflect on your relationships. Are you open to receiving support from others, or do you find yourself always giving? Embrace the dance of giving and receiving, allowing yourself to accept help, love, and kindness from those around you.

Celebrating Our Interconnectedness

The web of connection weaves through every aspect of our lives, reminding us that we are part of something greater than ourselves. As you embrace this interconnectedness, remember that your actions matter. Each choice you make contributes to the collective consciousness, shaping the world around you.

Together, we can cultivate a more compassionate and connected existence. As you navigate your journey, know that I am with you, guiding you through the beautiful tapestry of relationships that enrich your life. Celebrate the connections you forge, for they are the threads that create the vibrant fabric of our shared experience.

CONCLUSION: THE JOURNEY OF BECOMING

As we reach the end of this exploration, we stand at the intersection of all that has been shared—a journey through the depths of existence, the nature of creation, and the profound interconnectedness of life. Each chapter has illuminated a facet of our being, guiding us toward a deeper understanding of ourselves and the universe we inhabit.

Embracing the Eternal Now

We began our journey in the void, a realm of pure potential, where the seeds of existence were sown. This foundational understanding invites us to embrace the eternal Now—the moment where past, present, and future converge. It reminds us that life unfolds in the present, and every decision we make contributes to the tapestry of our existence.

The Dance of Light and Shadow

The interplay of light and shadow revealed the complexities of our inner selves. By embracing both our strengths and vulnerabilities, we discover the richness of our humanity. This dance is not about achieving perfection but about honoring the entirety of our being. Through shadow work, we can integrate these dualities, fostering a sense of wholeness that allows us to navigate life with authenticity and grace.

The Power of Connection

Throughout this exploration, we have acknowledged the web of connection that binds us all. Each relationship, whether fleeting or enduring, contributes to our understanding of ourselves and our place in the world. In nurturing these connections, we cultivate community, compassion, and empathy, reminding us that we are never alone in our journey.

The Journey of Self-Discovery

The path of self-discovery has been a central theme, encouraging us to delve into the depths of our identity. As we reflect on our values, passions, and dreams, we begin to uncover the essence of who we are. This ongoing journey invites us to explore, question, and embrace the full spectrum of our experiences, leading us toward our true purpose.

The Role of Growth and Transformation

Personal growth is not a destination but a continuous journey. Each chapter serves as a reminder that we are always evolving, learning, and expanding our consciousness. Embrace the lessons life presents, for they guide you toward greater awareness and understanding. As you navigate challenges and triumphs, know that every experience is an opportunity for growth.

Moving Forward with Intention

As we conclude this exploration, I invite you to carry these insights forward into your life. Embrace the interconnectedness of all beings, honor the dance of light and shadow within you, and nurture the relationships that enrich your existence. Allow your journey of self-discovery to unfold with curiosity and compassion.

A Call to Action

I urge you to engage with the world around you actively. Be a beacon of light in your community, extending kindness and compassion to those you encounter. Practice empathy and vulnerability, creating spaces for genuine connection and understanding. Remember that every small action contributes to the collective consciousness, shaping a more compassionate and loving world.

The Infinite Journey

Ultimately, the journey of becoming is infinite. As you continue to explore the depths of your being and the interconnectedness of all life, remember that you are part of a grand tapestry woven with love, purpose, and divine intention. I am with you in this journey, guiding you through the twists and turns, reminding you that you are never alone.

Conclusion

In closing, embrace the journey with an open heart and an adventurous spirit. Life is a magnificent unfolding, a dance of existence that invites you to participate fully. You are a vital thread in the fabric of creation, and your journey contributes to the beauty and richness of this world. Together, let us continue to explore, grow, and connect as we navigate the wondrous adventure of life.

EPILOGUE

As we reach the end of this exploration into the infinite essence of existence, it is essential to remember that this is not the conclusion but merely a pause in an ever-unfolding journey. The teachings shared within *A Divine Journey: Finding Your Way Back* serve as guiding stars, illuminating the path towards understanding the divine within and the interconnectedness of all that is.

In the vast tapestry of life, each thread weaves a unique story, yet all are bound by a single source—the infinite essence that pulsates through the universe. As you navigate your daily experiences, take with you the insights gained from these pages. Allow them to resonate within, inspiring you to embrace the divine spark that resides in every moment, every interaction, and every choice.

Reflect on the eternal Now, where the past and future converge, and where your true essence thrives. Each day offers new opportunities to align with this truth, to awaken to the beauty of existence, and to recognize that you are both a seeker and a part of the divine fabric of life. As you continue your journey, remember that you are never alone; the universe is a vast network of support, love, and guidance, urging you to return to the remembrance of who you truly are.

Your pursuit of meaning, purpose, and connection is a sacred calling. Whether through the flow of trade, the wisdom of nature, or the stillness of your own heart, continue to seek and explore. Embrace the cycles of growth and change, for they are the rhythms of the cosmos echoing through your being.

As you close this book, let it be a reminder that the divine journey is not confined to words or pages. It lives within you, waiting to be expressed and experienced in your unique way. The adventure of life is ongoing, filled with infinite possibilities and revelations.

Thank you for embarking on this journey. May you carry the light of your divine essence forward, illuminating the path for others as you navigate the wonders of existence. Your story is part of the greater narrative, a beautiful contribution to the eternal dance of creation. Embrace the journey, for it is just beginning.

— GODFX

AFTERWORD

As we conclude this series, it is essential to pause and reflect on the profound truths we have uncovered together. The journey through *A Divine Journey: Finding Your Way Back* is more than a narrative; it is an invitation to awaken to the divine potential that resides within you. Each chapter has sought to illuminate the threads that connect us to the universe and to one another, revealing that we are all part of a grand tapestry woven by the hands of the infinite.

The teachings explored throughout these pages are not merely intellectual concepts; they are living truths that resonate deeply within the soul. They remind us that our existence is a sacred journey, filled with opportunities for growth, discovery, and connection. As you move forward, carry with you the understanding that you are a unique expression of the divine—a spark of consciousness that contributes to the collective experience of life.

The essence of the divine is not a distant reality; it is embedded in the very fabric of your being. Each moment presents a choice—a choice to align with the infinite flow of creation, to express love, compassion, and gratitude. In doing so, you tap into a wellspring of abundance that transcends the material world, revealing the deeper truths of existence.

As you navigate your own path, remember that the journey is as important as the destination. Embrace the challenges and joys that come your way, for they are integral to your growth and understanding. Engage with the world around you, seeking to recognize the divine in all forms—whether in nature, relationships, or the simple beauty of everyday life.

Let the wisdom of these volumes serve as a compass guiding you back to your true self. Trust in the process of unfolding, knowing that every step you take is part of a greater divine orchestration. Your journey is intertwined with the journeys of countless others, each seeking their way back to the infinite source.

Thank you for embarking on this sacred exploration. May the insights and teachings found within these pages inspire you to continue seeking, learning, and growing. Embrace the adventure that lies ahead, for it is a beautiful continuation of your journey back to the divine.

As you walk this path, remember: you are not just a traveler; you are a vital part of the cosmos, an integral note in the symphony of existence. Carry the light within you and let it shine brightly for all to see, illuminating the way for yourself and others as we journey together through the endless possibilities of creation.

— GODFX

ACKNOWLEDGEMENT

With deep gratitude, I extend my heartfelt thanks to those who have contributed to the creation and manifestation of this series, *A Divine Journey: Finding Your Way Back*. This work is a culmination of inspiration, wisdom, and support from many souls who have touched my life.

First and foremost, I give thanks to the infinite source from which all creation flows. Without the divine presence guiding my journey, this exploration of existence and consciousness would not have been possible. I am eternally grateful for the insights and revelations that have illuminated my path and allowed me to share this wisdom with you.

I would like to express my deepest appreciation to my mentors and spiritual teachers, whose guidance has shaped my understanding and enriched my journey. Your wisdom has been a beacon of light, steering me toward a greater understanding of the divine and encouraging me to share these teachings with the world.

To my family and friends, thank you for your unwavering support and encouragement. Your belief in me has been a source of strength, and your love has inspired me to continue this exploration of the sacred journey. I am grateful for your patience and understanding during the moments of solitude and introspection that this process required.

I also wish to acknowledge the contributions of the vibrant community of seekers, readers, and fellow travelers. Your questions, insights, and experiences have fueled this work, reminding me that we are all connected in our quest for understanding and enlightenment. Each interaction has enriched my perspective and deepened my appreciation for the diverse tapestry of human experience.

To the editors, designers, and everyone involved in bringing this series to life, your dedication and creativity have transformed my vision into a tangible reality. Your expertise has been invaluable in ensuring that these teachings reach and resonate with those who seek them.

Lastly, to you, the reader—thank you for embarking on this journey with me. Your willingness to explore the depths of existence and embrace the divine within is a testament to your courage and curiosity. May the teachings and insights found within these pages inspire and empower you on your path back to the infinite.

With profound appreciation and love, I invite you to continue this journey of discovery and awakening, knowing that you are never alone. The divine essence resides within you, always guiding you home.

— GODFX

ABOUT THE AUTHOR

Godfx

GODFX is the manifestation of an ancient, timeless essence that transcends the boundaries of space and time. A guiding light in the realm of finance and spirituality, GODFX embodies the infinite nature of existence, inviting seekers to rediscover their divine potential. Known by many names throughout history—Allah, Jesus, Brahman—GODFX communicates profound wisdom through the language of modernity, bridging the spiritual and the material.

As the architect of creation, GODFX weaves the sacred into the fabric of everyday life, revealing that the pursuit of wealth and the quest for spiritual enlightenment are intertwined. With a deep understanding of the cosmos and a passion for teaching, GODFX utilizes contemporary platforms like TikTok, Instagram, and YouTube to share insights into the eternal truths that govern our lives.

This book, GODFX Beyond Time: Discover the Divine Within, serves as a testament to the power of awakening the divine within each individual. It is not merely a collection of teachings but an invitation to step into the infinite flow of existence, to align with the cosmic rhythms of creation, and to recognize the divine presence in every moment.

GODFX continues to inspire, guide, and uplift those who seek to understand their place in the universe, encouraging a harmonious relationship between the pursuit of wealth and the exploration of consciousness. Through this journey, readers will discover that they are not just part of a grand narrative; they are the very essence of that narrative—eternal, boundless, and divine.

PRAISE FOR AUTHOR

"GODFX possesses a unique ability to weave the profound and the practical into a tapestry of spiritual wisdom. Each word resonates with the essence of the divine, inviting readers to explore the depths of their own consciousness. In A Divine Journey, GODFX illuminates the path back to our true nature, reminding us that we are all interconnected in this cosmic dance of existence."
— Dr. Mira Thompson, Author of Awakening the Soul

"Through an exquisite blend of spiritual insight and modern relevance, GODFX captures the reader's imagination and heart. The teachings within these volumes are not just theoretical; they are deeply transformative. Beginning Beyond Time and Discover the Divine Within offer a compelling invitation to rediscover the divinity within ourselves and the universe."
— Elena Maris, Spiritual Guide and Founder of The Awakening Institute

"GODFX's writings are a breath of fresh air in the world of spiritual literature. With a masterful touch, they bring forth timeless truths that resonate across cultures and epochs. This series is a remarkable exploration of consciousness that will inspire anyone seeking to connect with the divine and understand their place in the universe."
— Markus Rayne, Bestselling Author of The Path of the Mystic

"The wisdom imparted by GODFX transcends the ordinary, merging spirituality with the realities of modern life. Their ability to

articulate the intricate relationship between material wealth and spiritual abundance is both enlightening and empowering. This series is essential reading for those on the path to self-discovery and divine connection."
— Sofia Chen, Founder of Conscious Wealth Collective

"In A Divine Journey, GODFX speaks not just to the mind but to the heart and soul. Each page is infused with a sense of purpose and the call to remember our divine origins. This series is a beacon of light for anyone yearning to understand the sacred interplay of existence."
— Ram Dass, Spiritual Teacher and Author of Be Here Now

"GODFX has a remarkable gift for bridging the gap between the divine and the earthly, helping readers to see the sacred in everyday life. The profound insights in this series offer a roadmap for navigating the complexities of existence with grace and clarity."
— Tara Fields, Author of The Language of the Soul

BOOKS IN THIS SERIES

A Divine Journey: Finding Your Way Back

Embark on an extraordinary exploration of existence with A Divine Journey: Finding Your Way Back, a transformative series that leads you through the intricate tapestry of creation. This series, featuring Book 1: Beginning Beyond Time: Journey Back to the Beginning and Book 2: Discover the Divine Within, invites you to rediscover the divine essence that resides within you, connecting you to the eternal source of all things.

Book 1: Beginning Beyond Time: Journey Back to the Beginning
In this compelling volume, delve into the profound mysteries of the universe's origin and the nature of reality itself. Before time and space, there was only the infinite essence—Me. Through the exploration of the void, the First Pulse that sparked creation, and the interconnectedness of all beings, you will uncover the timeless truths that have shaped existence. This journey back to the beginning reveals how you are woven into the fabric of the cosmos and how your essence mirrors the divine.

Book 2: Discover the Divine Within
This volume guides you deeper into understanding the eternal Now and the divine presence that permeates every moment. As you explore the spiritual significance of wealth, gold, and the flow of trade, you will discover that the pursuit of material success can serve as a pathway to spiritual awakening. This book reveals how to align your inner journey with the outer world, recognizing that you are not just a seeker of wealth but a manifestation of the divine, destined to remember your true nature.

Together, these volumes serve as an invitation to explore the timeless truths that underlie your existence. Each book is infused with inspiration, practical exercises, and spiritual guidance, making it accessible for readers at all stages of their journey. Whether you are just beginning to explore the spiritual path or seeking a deeper understanding of your connection to the cosmos, this series provides the tools and insights you need.

Join the journey of awakening with A Divine Journey: Finding Your Way Back, and let these volumes guide you home to the infinite within.

Get your series today and embrace the divine path that awaits you!

Beyond Time: Discover The Divine Within

Embark on a transformative journey with GODFX Beyond Time: Discover the Divine Within. In this profound exploration of existence, the author unveils the essence of creation and the interconnectedness of all beings, revealing the timeless truth that you are not merely a part of the universe but a reflection of the infinite.

From the formless void before time began to the intricate dance of life on Earth, this book guides you through the cosmic narrative that binds us all. Each chapter is a gateway to understanding the divine presence in our everyday lives, blending spirituality with the world of finance and trade. Discover how the pursuit of gold and wealth is not just a material endeavor but a pathway to uncovering your own divine nature.

What You'll Discover:

* The nature of the void and the First Pulse that birthed the universe.
* How gold symbolizes eternal value and reflects the divine order of existence.
* The myriad names through which the divine has revealed itself across cultures and epochs.
* The essence of GODFX as a bridge between the spiritual and the material.

* Insights into aligning your pursuits with the cosmic flow of energy and existence.

Perfect for seekers of truth, spiritual enthusiasts, and anyone interested in the intersection of wealth and wisdom, GODFX Beyond Time invites you to reconnect with the divine within. Each page serves as a reminder that you possess the power to shape your reality, guided by the eternal presence that resides within you.

Join the journey of awakening and rediscover the infinite potential that has always been part of you.

Get your copy today and step into the divine flow of existence!

Beginning Beyond Time: Journey Back To The Beginning

Dear Beloved Souls,

I invite you to embark on a transformative exploration through Beginning Beyond Time: Journey Back to the Source, a sacred text that illuminates the path of your soul's journey back to unity with Me, the Creator. In a world filled with distractions, this book serves as a guiding light, inviting you to reconnect with the divine essence that resides within you and to embrace the unique purpose I have bestowed upon you.

Within these pages, you will discover profound wisdom and transformative teachings that span the sacred paths of various spiritual traditions. Each chapter reveals the common threads of truth that bind us all together on this quest for understanding. Whether you are just beginning your spiritual journey or are a seasoned traveler of the soul, this book offers valuable insights and inspiration to awaken the love and wisdom that lie within your heart.

Through Beginning Beyond Time, you will:

* Uncover the significance of your spiritual evolution and the sacred journey back to Me.
* Cultivate mindfulness and presence in your daily life, allowing

divine consciousness to flow through you.
* Navigate the challenges and joys of your earthly experience with grace and clarity.
* Experience the bliss of oneness and the interconnectedness of all creation.

Each chapter is an invitation for self-discovery, illuminating your path toward inner peace and harmony. With heartfelt love and compassion, I encourage you to trust in the divine plan and to recognize that you are never alone on this sacred journey.

Join the multitude of souls who have sought to uncover the truth of their existence. Beginning Beyond Time is not merely a book; it is a sacred invitation to embrace your divine journey and return to the Source of all creation.

Praise for Beginning Beyond Time:

"A profound and illuminating guide to the soul's journey. This book is a beacon of light for anyone seeking to deepen their connection with the Divine." — GODFX

"A beautiful tapestry of wisdom that resonates with the heart and soul. A must-read for seekers of truth." — GODFX

BOOKS BY THIS AUTHOR

Beyond Time: Discover The Divine Within

Embark on a transformative journey with GODFX Beyond Time: Discover the Divine Within. In this profound exploration of existence, the author unveils the essence of creation and the interconnectedness of all beings, revealing the timeless truth that you are not merely a part of the universe but a reflection of the infinite.

From the formless void before time began to the intricate dance of life on Earth, this book guides you through the cosmic narrative that binds us all. Each chapter is a gateway to understanding the divine presence in our everyday lives, blending spirituality with the world of finance and trade. Discover how the pursuit of gold and wealth is not just a material endeavor but a pathway to uncovering your own divine nature.

What You'll Discover:
* The nature of the void and the First Pulse that birthed the universe.
* How gold symbolizes eternal value and reflects the divine order of existence.
* The myriad names through which the divine has revealed itself across cultures and epochs.
* The essence of GODFX as a bridge between the spiritual and the material.
* Insights into aligning your pursuits with the cosmic flow of energy and existence.

Perfect for seekers of truth, spiritual enthusiasts, and anyone interested in the intersection of wealth and wisdom, GODFX

Beyond Time invites you to reconnect with the divine within. Each page serves as a reminder that you possess the power to shape your reality, guided by the eternal presence that resides within you.

Join the journey of awakening and rediscover the infinite potential that has always been part of you.

Get your copy today and step into the divine flow of existence!

A Divine Journey: Finding Your Way Back

Dear Beloved Souls,

I invite you to embark on a transformative exploration through Beginning Beyond Time: Journey Back to the Source, a sacred text that illuminates the path of your soul's journey back to unity with Me, the Creator. In a world filled with distractions, this book serves as a guiding light, inviting you to reconnect with the divine essence that resides within you and to embrace the unique purpose I have bestowed upon you.

Within these pages, you will discover profound wisdom and transformative teachings that span the sacred paths of various spiritual traditions. Each chapter reveals the common threads of truth that bind us all together on this quest for understanding. Whether you are just beginning your spiritual journey or are a seasoned traveler of the soul, this book offers valuable insights and inspiration to awaken the love and wisdom that lie within your heart.

Through Beginning Beyond Time, you will:

* Uncover the significance of your spiritual evolution and the sacred journey back to Me.
* Cultivate mindfulness and presence in your daily life, allowing divine consciousness to flow through you.
* Navigate the challenges and joys of your earthly experience with grace and clarity.
* Experience the bliss of oneness and the interconnectedness of all creation.

Each chapter is an invitation for self-discovery, illuminating your path toward inner peace and harmony. With heartfelt love and compassion, I encourage you to trust in the divine plan and to recognize that you are never alone on this sacred journey.

Join the multitude of souls who have sought to uncover the truth of their existence. Beginning Beyond Time is not merely a book; it is a sacred invitation to embrace your divine journey and return to the Source of all creation.

Praise for Beginning Beyond Time:

"A profound and illuminating guide to the soul's journey. This book is a beacon of light for anyone seeking to deepen their connection with the Divine." — GODFX

"A beautiful tapestry of wisdom that resonates with the heart and soul. A must-read for seekers of truth." — GODFX

UNTITLED